# The Agent in the Agency
## *Media, Popular Culture, and Everyday Life in America*

THE HAMPTON PRESS COMMUNICATION SERIES
Popular Culture
John A. Lent, series editor


The Agent in the Agency: Media, Popular Culture, and Everday Life in America
*Arthur Asa Berger*

Jewish Jesters: A Study in American Popular Comedy
*Arthur Asa Berger*

Indian Popular Cinema: Industry, Ideology, and Consciousness
*Manjunath Pendakur*

*forthcoming*

Advertising and Everyday Life
*Neil Alperstein*

Cartooning in Africa
*John Lent (ed.)*

Cartooning in Latin America
*John Lent (ed.)*

Serial Monogamy: Soap Opera, Lifespan, and the Gendered Politics of Fantasy
*Christine Scodari*

# The Agent in the Agency
*Media, Popular Culture, and Everyday Life in America*

Arthur Asa Berger
San Francisco State University

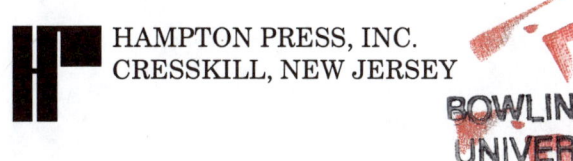

HAMPTON PRESS, INC.
CRESSKILL, NEW JERSEY

Copyright © 2003 by Hampton Press, Inc.

All rights reserved. No part of this publication may be reproduced, stored in a retrieval system, or transmitted in any form or by any means, electronic, mechanical, photocopying, microfilming, recording, or otherwise, without permission of the publisher.

Printed in the United States of America

**Library of Congress Cataloging-in-Publication Data**

Arthur Asa Berger, 1933-
   The agent in the agency: media, popular culture, and everyday life in America / Arthur Asa Berger
      p. cm. -- (The Hampton Press communication series. Popular culture)
   Includes bibliographical references and indexes.
   ISBN 1-57273-494-9 (alk. paper) -- ISBN 1-57273-495-7 (pbk: alk. paper)
   1. Popular culture--United States. 2. Mass media--United States--Social life and customs--1971-. I. Title. II. Series

E169.04 B465 2002
306'.0973--dc21

                                              2002027281

Hampton Press, Inc.
23 Broadway
Cresskill, NJ 07626

# Contents

Preface

## PART I: THEORETICAL CONCERNS

**1 How Did You Become Yourself?**   3
*How Do We Become Ourselves? 4
Repetition Compulsion 5
The Meanings of the Term Popular 6
The Meanings of the Term Culture 8
Falling Off the Map: How Cultures Differ 10
An Average American's Typical Day of Media Usage 12*

**2 The Impact of Popular Culture on Personality**   15
*On the Power of Metaphor: It's All in the Game 16
On the Power of Identification With Symbolic Heroes,
   Heroines, and Celebrities 18
Mimesis or Imitation 19
Mimetic Desire 21
Models We Imitate 22
The Power of Images and Style 22
The Power of Information 23
The Power of Stories 24
The Power of Spectacles: The Super Bowl 29*

　　　　*How Concepts Are Defined and How They Affect Us* 29
　　　　*The Power of Music* 30
　　　　*Conclusions* 32

**3　The Power of Groups**　　　　　　　　　　　　　　　　　33
　　　　*Political Cultures* 34
　　　　*Taste Cultures* 37
　　　　*Postmodernism and Popular Culture* 41

## PART II: APPLICATIONS

**4　Speculations on a Spectacle: The Super Bowl**　　　　47
　　　　*A Confession From an Ex-Sportswriter* 47
　　　　*A Defamiliarized Perspective on Super Bowl XXXII:*
　　　　　*A Report From a Martian Anthropologist to the*
　　　　　*Martian Public* 48
　　　　*Linguistic Analysis* 49
　　　　*A Marxist Perspective on the Super Bowl* 50
　　　　*The Super Bowl as a Sign System: A Semiotic*
　　　　　*Perspective* 52
　　　　*Psychoanalytic Perspectives on the Super Bowl* 53
　　　　*Sociological Aspects of the Super Bowl* 54
　　　　*Conclusions: A Point After* 55

**5　Frasier: A 20th-Century Fool**　　　　　　　　　　　　57
　　　　*Why We Laugh* 57
　　　　*What Makes Us Laugh* 58
　　　　*Applying the Technique to "The Good Son"* 59

**6　Bloopers: What They Are and What They Mean**　　67
　　　　*Kinds of Bloopers* 67
　　　　*Why We Laugh at Bloopers* 68
　　　　*Bloopers as a Form of Liberation* 69
　　　　*A Personal Note From a Lover of Bloopers* 70
　　　　*Enjoy, Enjoy* 70
　　　　*The Ethical Problem* 71
　　　　*Bloopers About History* 72
　　　　*Bloopers About Religion* 73
　　　　*Bloopers About Science* 74
　　　　*Bloopers on Literature and Art* 75

*Bloopers on Philosophy and Philosophical Concerns  76*
  *Bloopers on Health and Well-Being  77*
  *Bloopers About Politics  78*
  *Bloopers That Are Definitions  79*

**7   Decoding Everyday Life**                                     **81**
  *Cigarette Smoking  81*
  *Traffic Signals  84*
  *Pathways and Oppositions in the Supermarket  87*
  *Codes in the Classroom: Exclusivity Encourages
    Passivity  89*

**8   The Agent in the Agency**                                    **93**
  *The Agent in the Agency I: (1973) In Search of the
    Quintessential Englishman  122*
  *The Agent in the Agency II: Days of Whites and Roses
    (and a Bit of Cognac)  130*
  *The Agent in the Agency III: "We Only Give People
    What They Want!?"  133*

**9   Writing My Dissertation on *Li'l Abner***
                                                                   **137**
**10  Conclusions: Survivors of *Survivor* and Other Pop
    Culture Crazes**                                               **143**

References                                                         147

Suggested Readings                                                 149

Index                                                              161

# *Preface*

## HOW I BECAME A SECRET AGENT

In the early 1970s, George Gerbner, who was at the time the editor of *The Journal of Communication*, asked me to write an article about what I did when I analyzed popular culture. Being young and very serious, I wrote a long essay—it was something like 40 pages long. He lopped off the first 32 pages and only used the last segment of my article, called "The Secret Agent." In this section of the article I suggested that analyzing popular culture was like being a secret agent.

You spend your time, I wrote, looking for "secrets" hidden in popular culture—insights into values and beliefs found in everything from comic strips to soap operas, from sitcoms to football games, from fads to ads. After my article was published, I adopted the comic persona of the secret agent, and spent 40 years snooping around various aspects of popular culture, looking for "secrets." In this book, you can see some of the products of my secret agentry. For example, I offer a report, "The Agent in the Agency," which is really an ethnography that deals with what I learned when I spent 3 weeks at an advertising agency in San Francisco (and a few weeks at an advertising agency in London 30 years ago) looking for insights into advertising and trying to figure out how advertising works.

In this preface, I introduce myself and offer several offbeat interpretations of American popular culture that I made in earlier years. There are some scholars—who I would describe as ultra-serious social scientists—who have suggested that I am not a secret agent but a "put-on" artist and that most of my ideas should not really be taken seriously. I hope my readers won't be put off by such notions. I do, I confess, sometimes have a bit of fun and push ideas to rather strange conclusions, but what I am offering, I argue, are insights that explain all kinds of things and make connections between phenomena that often were not recognized before. That's what secret agents do.

## THE EVANGELICAL HAMBURGER

In 1964, I wrote an article arguing that McDonald's was an "evangelical hamburger" that would eventually spread its golden arches all over the world. I added that it was deluding people into thinking, by a process I called *hambourgeoisment,* that their access to cheap ground meat meant they were middle class. (That is, I argued, the dynamics of the McDonald's organization and its outlets resembled the dynamics of many evangelical religions.)

A friend of mine, familiar with my work, told me he thought this idea was crazy. He suggested that I made everything up as I went along and merely threw occasional charts and diagrams into my articles and books to trick sociologists (a matter rather easily done, so it seems).

## PHILOSOPHICAL PERSPECTIVES ON ADVERTISING:

I suggest that my friend (like many others in academia, it turns out) didn't consider me to be a serious scholar because I spent so much time writing about popular culture and the mass media. I had written an article about deodorants with a whimsical title, "I Stink, Therefore I Am," suggesting that our passion to remove body odor was tied, ultimately, to Puritanism, perfectionism, and an unconscious and unrecognized fear of death.

In the same vein, I had speculated, in an essay called "To Buy Is To Be Perceived" (playing upon the philosopher Berkeley's famous dictum "to be is to be perceived"), that most of us lead lives, not only of "quiet desperation" but also of relative anonymity and that, generally speaking, it is only when we purchase things that anyone pays much attention to us. Thus, we buy things to prove to ourselves, ultimately, that we exist. And when sales people do acknowledge our existence, it is only pro forma. We get few personal letters nowadays, and need the bills in the mail to remind ourselves (prove to ourselves?) that we do, in fact, exist.

## THE TV-GUIDED AMERICAN

I must confess—a considerable number of sociologists, anthropologists, psychologists, culture critics, and others haven't liked my theories, my articles, my books, and my work, in general. Some of them don't like me, either. I had written a book, *The TV-Guided American,* which was published in the mid-1970s. The book was reviewed by a critic in *The New York Times.* It concluded with the line, "Berger is to the study of television what Idi Amin is to tourism in Uganda." Since Idi Amin was killing thousands of people in Uganda, at the time, it was not a compliment. This reviewer, who was not a scholar, did not take kindly to my use of psychoanalytic theories and semiotics to analyze television.

This is a typical layperson's response to works by scholars, which often has a great deal of "arcane" language and is based on obscure theories. But complicated thinking, I would suggest, often requires complicated language, even though some writers and scholars overdo things, I must admit.

In the book that follows, you will not find too many (I hope) extravagant analyses or too much arcane language. In the first part of the book, I deal with theoretical matters relevant to the study of popular culture and offer a number of concepts to be used in analyzing popular culture. Then, in the second part, I interpret a number of important kinds of popular culture—everything from the Super Bowl to bloopers to *Frasier,* the brilliant situation comedy. I also offer an extended ethnography that describes what life (if people who work in advertising agencies actually have lives) in advertising agencies is like. That ethnography provides the title of the book—I was, literally and figuratively, a "secret" agent in an agency.

I hope you will find my book both entertaining and edifying and that you will approach popular culture and the mass media, in the future, with a more discriminating sensibility and with an awareness of the role popular culture plays in your life and in society.

## ACKNOWLEDGMENTS

I would like to thank everyone at the advertising agencies I visited (the one in England will not be named and the one in San Francisco is Goldberg Moser O'Neill—GMO) for their hospitality and many kindnesses. I learned a great deal from my experiences at these agencies and hope that the people at these agencies will not feel that I have given away any valuable secrets or abused their confidence in any way. I offer my ethnography of these two agencies—one from 1974 and one from 1999—in the hope that readers will gain some interesting insights into the advertising industry. I must confess to a sense of ambivalence about advertising. I am impressed by the creativity of people in the industry and full of anxiety about their power. As Fred Goldberg, the head of GMO once said to me, "even bad advertising works." I also want to thank my editor, John Lent, and my publisher, Barbara Bernstein, for being so supportive of my efforts.

—*Arthur Asa Berger*

# Part I

*Theoretical Concerns*

# Chapter 1

# *How Did You Become Yourself?*

In this chapter, I deal with the relation between culture and our personal identities by discussing how we define culture and, in particular, an important kind of culture, *popular culture*. What culture is and how it affects our personalities and identities is a controversial subject. I offer some considerations that relate to the culture question and more specifically, how culture, popular culture and identity may be related to one another. I discuss the following topics:

1. How we become ourselves.
2. Repetition compulsion and its connection to our immersion in popular culture.
3. The various meanings of the term *popular*.
4. The various meanings of the term *culture*.
5. Travel literature as a means of reflecting cultural differences and national identities.

I start with that most fascinating of questions—How do we become ourselves? How do we achieve an identity? Because identity is a preoccupation of just about everyone in this postmodern age, you might ask yourself, "How did I become the person I am" and think about this question as you read this material.

## HOW DO WE BECOME OURSELVES?

It's an interesting question. How did you become yourself? Someone from France once asked me, "What was your *formation*?" That term, *formation,* suggests that people don't create themselves as much as may think they do. What happens, instead, is that they are "formed" in some way and to varying degrees by the culture in which they grow up, by the circumstances of their birth (including their birth order), their gender, their family, their religion, the town or city where they were born and the state (in America) or the country in which they were raised, the language they learned, their education, and countless other variables.

If we all find ourselves, as Mannheim (1936) suggested in *Ideology and Utopia*, shaped, or perhaps even predetermined, by a "ready-made situation" when we are born and "preformed patterns of thought and conduct" when we grow up, how do we achieve some kind of a distinctive identity?

As a wit once said, "the idea of the self-made man (and now we would add woman) relieves God of a lot of responsibility." And it does!

There is also the matter of our inborn (physical, genetic, whatever you wish to call them) natures—the attributes of our selves that are "hard-wired," so to speak, in people. I have two children and they are as different as night and day. How does one explain this? Well, for one thing, one is a female (the firstborn) and the other is a male. So there is birth order and gender to consider. But they each have radically different personalities and interests, and these differences stem to a considerable degree, I would say, from their basic natures. It may all stem from their genes? There was something in each of them, I would suggest, that is tied to their different intrinsic selves and cannot be explained by gender, birth order, where they grew up, and so on. My point, then, is that we have to give nature her due in the so-called "nature–nurture" debate. But only to a point.

Nurture plays a big role, too.

I often ask my students—"How did you become yourselves?" What I mean by that question is—how did you end up becoming the person you are? One student once looked at me with a puzzled expression on his face. Then he said, "I don't know—I was just lucky, I guess." And that probably is the way most of us feel about ourselves. "We were just lucky!"

But maybe, in some respects, we weren't. We might not have been lucky as far as the family into which we were born (which affects our life chances) or in terms of our genetic makeup or in any number of other respects, such as what we look like, what our personalities are like, where we live, and what popular music, television shows, and films we like. In the discussion that follows, I use the concept *repetition compulsion*, which I believe might help explain our collective addiction (and mine, as well) to the media and popular culture.

## REPETITION COMPULSION

Sigmund Freud used the term *repetition compulsion* to explain the behavior of certain individuals who cannot help repeating certain of their earlier experiences, most of which generally were painful. This concept is best understood as involving the active repetition of something unpleasant that was experienced, an experience that is generally connected to some kind of trauma. Repetition compulsion is often seen in the play of children, who continually repeat actions related to bad experiences they have had in order to find a way to cope with them.

I mention this matter of repetition compulsion for two reasons. First, on the personal level, I wonder whether my career of writing about popular culture and the media, for almost 40 years, has an element of repetition compulsion in it. Is there something in my psyche that makes me write about popular culture and the media over and over again—in different books with different emphases, mind you—but still, the same general subject?

I keep on writing about popular culture because I keep finding new things and new ways to write about it. In part this is because popular culture is such a large, amorphous, hard to define and pin down, hard to come to grips with and explain, subject. There's always something new to think about. You think you've seen everything and then CBS broadcasts *Survivor*.

Someone once suggested that all writers write the same book, over and over again, but in different ways. So my fascination with the subject of popular culture and the media and my inability to escape from it, may be due to the fact that I am a writer and all my books are, in some vague way, variation of some basic or generic Berger book. I became interested in popular culture because I had the sense that it plays a major role in socializing people, that it— more than many other things—is what helps us, if help is the correct word—as individuals and to some degree collectively—become what we are.

I saw an article in a Sunday supplement recently that was titled "Parents Come in Third: Genes and Peers are Basic." One question that comes to mind, of course, is how did those peers who have such mysterious powers over the lives of our children become the persons they became? How did those peers, who allegedly influence us, and especially our children, so much, arrive at themselves?

If I were to ask you, "how did you become yourself?" after you said "I was lucky, I guess," I'd probe deeper and probably find that popular culture and the mass media played a major role in giving you ideas about yourself and about life. Popular culture helped teach you how you were supposed to relate to others and how to decide what is important in life—or as the European who asked me about myself would put it, popular culture played a major role in your formation.

The second aspect of repetition compulsion that interests me involves the enormous amount of media Americans consume on a daily basis. Is there some element of repetition compulsion in each of us that is behind all the radio we listen to, the television we watch, the music we hear or play for ourselves on our stereo systems, the comics and newspapers and magazines we read, the video games we play? The average American listens to the radio for more than 1 hour each day, watches television for around 4 hours each day, plays video games for varying amounts of time, and spends another hour or two reading newspapers, magazines, books, and so on. So, I ask—are we using the media—without recognizing what we are doing, of course—to help us deal with some traumas we experienced and have forgotten about, some problems we face, or some unconscious anxieties and desires we have? Repetition compulsion involves, let us remember, the unconscious. We are seldom aware of the roots of our behavior. And although we may recognize, at times, some kind of a habitual (or even compulsive) nature to our behavior, we are not, as a rule, aware that the causes of our behavior—if the psychoanalysts are correct—are buried deep in our psyches.

## THE MEANINGS OF THE TERM *POPULAR*

The term *popular* is a rather complicated one; almost as complicated as the term *culture,* which I discuss shortly. Popular comes from the Latin term *popularis*, which means "people." There are several meanings connected with the term *popular*: first, involving the people in general; second, suitable for the people (in that sense that it is easy to comprehend); third, having widespread acceptance or appeal.

A thesaurus offers a number of other aspects of the term such as: "approved," "beloved," "common," "customary," "desired," "famous," "fashionable," "lay," "prevalent," "public," and "usual." And for the related term *popularize,* it suggests "explain," "vulgarize," and "make understandable." We see, then, that popular contains a number of different meanings.

When many, if not most, critics write about popular culture, they tend to use it in a negative sense—works of art that are easy to understand, that cater to the so-called "lowest common denominator," that are often vulgar, trite, formulaic, sexist, and superficial. A number of years ago I wrote an article that was titled "Why is Popular Culture So Unpopular?" My point was that popular culture is "unpopular" with elites who tend to look down on the public and particularly on public taste in art, literature, film, and theater. Popular culture is, of course, very popular with the general public (or "populace") for whom it is created.

What is important to understand is that criticism of popular culture on the taste level will almost always find it inferior to "elite" works of art; that's a given, most of the time. Popular culture is worth studying because of its role in shaping our identities, in giving people ideas about what's good and bad, what's beautiful and ugly, what's important and trivial. That is, we study popular culture because of its role in socializing and enculturating people, because of what it reflects about culture and society (or about subcultures and other groups of people) and because, in addition, it affects culture and society in profound ways. Popular culture also has played a role in shaping so-called "elite" culture so there are even aesthetic reasons for investigating popular culture. And, of course, some popular culture is aesthetically satisfying, too. It isn't all junk—although most of it is!

In the following discussion, I suggest (in a somewhat oversimplified way) the differences between popular culture—that is, popular works of art or mass-mediated works of art—and elite works of art as elite critics see things. To make things simple, we can think of two works: Shakespeare's *Hamlet* and the film *Wayne's World.* I am taking two extreme examples to make my point and to clarify things. But we could do the same even with less extreme examples.

*Wayne's World* is mass-produced, mass-mediated, appeals to the mythical lowest common denominator, is relatively simple-minded, had a short life and offers little insight into human nature. *Hamlet,* on the other hand, is the work of an individual playwright, is not mass-mediated as a rule (although film versions of the play have continued to be made), is for refined sensibilities, is timeless, is incredibly complex, and offers brilliant insights into human nature . . . which is why it continues to interest us 400 years after it was written.

I realize, of course, that I have taken extreme texts (the term critics use for plays, movies, poems, comic books, advertisements, and videos) to make my point. If we make a film of *Hamlet* and it is shown is movie houses, then later on television, we have what was originally an elite text shown in a mass medium. Does that mean it is now popular culture?

In the last few decades, our attitudes about films have changed. When they were "movies" they were seen as popular culture; when they became "film" (as in "art films") and "cinema," they were seen as works that could be popular culture but also could be of elite culture. The point is, a given medium can be used for both popular and elite culture. It's not the medium that's crucial—it is the text! Since I have used the term *culture* a good deal, it is worth considering the various meanings of *culture*. After all, as I pointed out earlier, popular culture is a kind of culture!

## THE MEANINGS OF THE TERM *CULTURE*

Culture is one of the more complicated words we deal with here. One of the problems we encounter is that there are a number of different meanings attached to the term. As I suggested earlier, we think of culture two ways: first, in terms of aesthetic matters (relative to the arts) and second, as a concept used by anthropologists to describe a people's way of life. There are more than 100 different definitions of culture used by anthropologists, so I understand.

The word *culture* comes from the Latin cultus, which means "care" and from the French colere, which means "to till" as in "till the ground." There are a number of words associated with culture. For example, there is the term *cult,* which suggests something religious or sacred . . . and lately, something menacing and dangerous. We are continually amazed at the power cults have to shape people's behavior, to brainwash them—to turn intelligent and educated people into fanatics. Here we are dealing with the power of charismatic personalities and of groups over individuals. If cults can exercise enormous power over individuals and groups of people, can't we say that cultures also can do the same thing, although not to as extreme a degree?

There is also the term *cultivated,* which means either growing something or, in the realm of aesthetics and the arts, sophisticated taste. Just as plants only exist because they are cared for by some cultivator, over a period of time, so people's taste and cultivation only are developed by education and training. It takes time to develop a refined sensibility, to become discriminating, to appreciate texts that are difficult and complex and not immediately satisfying.

Bacteriologists also speak about cultures, but they use the term to describe the bacteria that grow in Petri dishes if they are given suitable media (sources of nourishment). This matter of bacteria growing in media may be an important metaphor for us: Just as bacteria need media to grow into cultures, so do human beings need cultures to survive and develop themselves. We don't do it all on our own—even though there is much talk of individualism (a concept we learn from our cultures) and the so-called self-made man and woman, mentioned earlier.

There are interesting parallels that can be drawn between bacteriology and anthropology. Bacteriology deals with bacteria that are grown in media and that form cultures. Anthropology deals with humans who are affected by media and who form cultures.

Of course we are much more complex than bacteria; in truth, each of us form a kind of medium for countless kinds of bacteria and minute bugs that inhabit our mouths and various other parts of our bodies. Bacteriology involves the cultivation and study of microorganisms (bacteria) in prepared nutrients and the study of media or mass-mediated culture (what is often called cultural criticism nowadays) involves the study of individuals and groups in a predominantly, but not completely, mass-mediated culture.

Let me offer a typical anthropological definition of culture. Culture involves socially acquired behavior patterns found in humans that are typically communicated by means of symbols of one kind of another. Culture therefore involves language, the arts, science, our legal systems, and the material objects we create such as tools, machines, houses and other kinds of buildings.

Let's consider some of these topics:

1. *Behavior patterns*. We are talking about codes and patterns of behavior here that are found in groups of people.
2. *Socially acquired*. We are taught these behavior patterns as we grow up in a family in some geographical location and are profoundly affected by the family we are born into, its religion, and all kinds of other matters.
3. *Transmitted by means of symbols*. This refers to language and works of art, both of which have a profound impact on our psyches and our consciousness. It also can be

understood to refer to communication of all kinds and involving all media: spoken words, facial expression, mass mediated texts, and so on.
4. *The distinctive achievements of human groups.* This is important because it points out that it is in groups that we become human and become enculturated or acculturated (two words for the same thing, for all practical purposes). We each have our own distinctive natures but we are also part of society.
5. *Artifacts in which cultural achievements are embodied.* The artifacts we are talking about here are the popular culture texts carried in the various media and other nonmediated aspects of popular culture (or not directly mediated) such as fashions in clothes, food, artifacts (what anthropologists call "material culture"), language use, sexual practices, and related matters. We know that a lot of our popular culture, although not carried by the media, is nevertheless profoundly affected by it.

We can see, then, that popular culture is a very complicated matter that plays some kind of a role in shaping our consciousness and our behavior. When I say "our" behavior, I mean my behavior and your behavior. You may think you are immune from the impact of the media and popular culture, but that is a delusion that is generated, I would suggest, by the media.

We may think we are not affected by the media and popular culture (sometimes called mass-mediated culture) but we are wrong. We must make a distinction between affected by and determined by here. Popular culture affects us but it doesn't necessarily determine every act we do . . . although some scholars, who believe the media are very powerful, might argue with this point.

## FALLING OFF THE MAP: HOW CULTURES DIFFER

For a graphic example of how cultures differ, let me offer two descriptions of different places by the Indian travel writer Pico Iyer (1993). They come from his book *Falling Off the Map: Some Lonely Places of the World,* a collection of travel articles about seldom-visited places (by American travelers, at least) he wrote for various publications.

I'll start with his description of Saigon, which he called "wild," and where he counted, one evening, more than 100 two-wheel vehicles racing by him in jam-packed streets in the course of 1 minute. He went to a dance club where he found a large number of gay boys wearing sleeveless t-shirts dancing to David Byrne's music. When he left, he was solicited by various women asking him if he would like a special massage or wanted a souvenir. Around midnight he saw a horde of taxi girls stream out of the clubs in their party dresses and ride off in scooters, which they had parked in front of the hotels on "Simultaneous Uprising" street. Inside the hotels, delegates to a fair trade conference huddled, gazing at the legion of mini-skirted girls, while the girls offered their services for oral sex and boys bargained with tourists for access to their sisters. The experience, he says, is Fellini-esque, as beautiful women in golden ao dais waved from slowly moving motorbikes. Compare this description of Saigon with his portrait of Reykjavik, Iceland, equally as fascinating and fantastic but considerably different from Saigon.

Iceland, he says, is bewildering and hard to comprehend. It has the largest number of presses and readers, per capita, of any country in the world. Reykjavik, a small city, has five daily newspapers, and publishes an enormous number of books on a per capita basis. To match Iceland's literary production, the United States would have to publish 1,200 new books each day. Iceland's language is the oldest living language in Europe. Approximately three of every four eldest children in Iceland are illegitimate. Because every son of a man named Kristjan is called Kristjansson, and every daughter Kristjansdottir, the surnames of mothers are always different from their children. The president of Iceland is, Iyer says, just another beautiful blonde single mother and the Parliament building, a small house is just a few doors down from the Salvation Army hotel.

We can see that there are considerable differences between Saigon and Reykjavik, although just to be fair, Iyer pointed out the incredible differences between cities in Vietnam, such as the differences between Saigon and Hue. Iyer's description of the landscape of Iceland may help explain the national character of the Icelanders. As he explains, Iceland didn't allow beer to be consumed until 1987 and there is no television on Thursdays. There are hardly any trees in Iceland and no vegetables. Iceland, he added, is an "ungodly wasteland." It is a land of tundras and volcanoes—a country that is so barren and forbidding that the NASA astronauts trained there.

There has to be some influence of this remarkable landscape and climate, of the Iceland geographical location, the amount of light and darkness in which people live, on the people who live there. In the same light, there has to be some influence of the jungle and the climate of Vietnam on its people.

What we become is, it seems to me, due to some curious combination of factors involving our natures (that is, the hard-wired elements of our personalities) and our cultures, with the matter of chance playing a big role as well. Think, for example, how different our lives would be if we had AIDS or were born with a severe "deformity." A baby born in Saigon but raised in Reykjavik would be considerably different when he or she grew up than a baby born in Reykjavik but raised in Saigon—in everything from preferences for foods, attitudes toward sex, languages spoken and understood, and other matters. Where we are located on some map when we are growing up, it turns out, plays an important role in our lives.

So culture makes a difference. And popular culture is the aspect of culture or kind of culture or manifestation of culture that seems to have the most immediate impact on us. Consider, for example, the amount of popular culture we are exposed to and involved with in our daily lives. I offer a hypothetical example—the story of an average American's typical day.

## AN AVERAGE AMERICAN'S TYPICAL DAY OF MEDIA USAGE

Let's return to the media usage in a typical day in a typical American—in this case, a fictional American, Johnny Q. Public, who is representative of many Americans. In the morning, he is awakened by a clock radio and he listens to the radio while he gets dressed. And then he has breakfast. He may also read the morning newspaper for a while. While he drives to work, he probably listens to the radio, also (if he is not busy talking on his cell phone, that is). This "drive-time" period probably lasts around 30 to 45 minutes, each way. Thus, it is reasonable to assume somewhere between 1.5 and 2 hours of radio listening on an average day. Johnny may have a job where he can listen to the radio, in which case the amount of listening he does balloons up to around 10 hours a day.

If he is an average television viewer, he watches almost 4 hours a day. This means, if he works from 9 a.m. to 5 p.m. and gets home at 6 p.m. and goes to bed at 11 p.m., 4 of those 5 hours are devoted to watching television. He may, of course, watch television in the morning, just after he gets up. That may take up part of his 4 hours. In addition, during a typical day, Johnny reads a newspaper for a while, looks at some magazines, may read for a while, and also listen to some music. It is possible that he reads a magazine while he listens to music on his stereo (or the radio) or while he "watches" television.

The following list shows the typical media usage of Americans, based on statistics obtained on the Internet:

- He/she spends 4.4 hours a day watching television—*that's 1,595 hours a year.*
- He/she spends 2.9 hours a day listening to the radio—*that's some 1,060 hours a year.*
- He/she spends 45 minutes a day listening to recorded music—*275 hours a year.*
- He/she spends 27 minutes a day reading newspapers—*about 165 hours a year.*
- He/she spends 17 minutes a day reading books—*approximately 103 hours a year.*
- He/she spends 14 minutes a day reading magazines—*some 85 hours a year.*

This comes to more than 8 hours of exposure to media and popular culture in a typical day. Obviously, this is an enormous amount of time in which we are involved with, immersed in, exposed to—whatever you wish to call it—popular culture, especially in its mass-mediated form. Is it possible that our exposure to all this popular culture and mass media has no effect on us? The question now arises—How does this popular culture affect us? It is that question I consider in the next chapter.

# Chapter 2

# *The Impact of Popular Culture on Personality*

The topics covered in this chapter all involve the various ways that popular culture may affect our minds, psyches, personalities, and behavior. I discuss the following topics:

1. Metaphor and the role of analogies.
2. The power of identification with symbolic heroes and heroines (and celebrities).
3. Mimesis—the power of imitation.
4. Mimetic desire: our imitation of the *desire* of others.
5. Models we imitate consciously and unconsciously.
6. The power of images.
7. The power of information.
8. The power of stories (narratives).
9. The power of spectacles.
10. How concepts work and affect us.
11. The power of music.

Is it possible that we can be immersed in popular culture to the extent that we are without being affected, in rather profound ways, by it? There are some critics who argue that our exposure to media and popular culture is not terribly important. Yes, we watch lots of television and yes, we listen to the radio a great deal, and yes, we listen to music on our stereos for hours and hours, and yes, we go to many movies and maybe we read a goodly number of comic books, murder mysteries, science fiction, and other popular fiction, but no, the impact of all of this popular culture is, in the end, short-lived and trivial.

I offer some considerations here that suggest the media have more powerful and longer lasting effects on individuals and on societies.

## ON THE POWER OF METAPHOR: IT'S ALL IN THE GAME

Metaphors are figures of speech that involve comparisons between two things. We find metaphors in poetry, where poets write "my love is a red rose." In metaphor, the comparison is very strong: There is an equal sign between two things: my love = a red rose. There is a weaker form of metaphor, called simile, in which a comparison is made using *like* or *as*. Here we find phrases such as "my love is *like* a red rose" or "my love is *as* a red rose."

What we have to realize is that these comparisons are important, not trivial matters. I say that because there is good reason to argue that metaphor has a major role in shaping our thinking and our behavior. Thus, in *Metaphors We Live By*, George Lakoff and Mark Johnson (1980) explained that although most people believe they have little involvement with metaphors in their lives, in actuality metaphors pervade their lives and are involved with not only language and our conceptual systems but also our thoughts and our actions. These concepts shape our everyday activities at the most mundane level.

Their book points out the important role metaphoric thinking plays in our lives—even though we may not recognize that our thinking is metaphoric or that there is a link between metaphor, our thinking, and our behavior.

But our behavior is connected to the ideas we have about how we should behave and what we have learned from our culture about how we should behave. Thus, let me offer an example. Let's take a song that I used to listen to, over and over again, when I was growing up: "All in the Game." The metaphor in this song is that love is a game. (This is much stronger than using a simile and saying love is like a game.) If love is a game, it means that loving involves playing a game, so to speak. And what are some of the characteristics of games? Let me suggest some of them:

1. *People cheat in games*. Not everyone plays fair in games and likewise, if love is a game, we shouldn't expect people

involved in a love affair to be fair. We know that people often do "cheat" on their lovers—but is this behavior to be expected or condoned? It seems that half the country western songs one hears are about lovers who cheat on one another or who have "cheating hearts."

2. *Games end after a while.* Games don't last forever, and thus love should be seen as something that one plays for a while, but terminates when one is bored with the game or for some other reason. If we see love as a game that is destined to end, it colors our notion of how to relate to our lovers. Does this mean we "use" lovers and then dump them when we're tired of the game?

3. *There are winners and losers in games.* What does it mean to "lose" in the game of love? Or "win" in love? This notion, that there are winners and losers, suggests that love is, somehow, a battle between rivals, each intent on winning. That is, love involves fighting for dominance and one party will be dominant and the other party ends up as submissive.

4. *Games have rules.* In order to play a game, there have to be mutually accepted rules that govern the game. But who determines what the rules of "love" are and how one interprets them? We learn about love from our exposure to popular culture, among other things. All we hear, hour after hour, on the radio are songs about love and these songs contain ideas and metaphors that give us our ideas about the nature of love.

5. *Games often take place in certain locations.* We play many games on boards (such as Monopoly) or fields (such as football and basketball) that help shape the games. Thus, there is some question about where we play the "game" of love? In restaurants? In bedrooms? And do we make a distinction between "love" and "sex" and if so, what is the difference?

6. *Games involve strategy and deception.* If love is a game, then logic tells us it is acceptable to use deception and various strategies to "win" the game—however we may define winning.

These points all suggest that the metaphor "love is a game" has logical implications that may have a profound influence on the way people think about love and the way they act when they are involved in love affairs. What makes the power of metaphor so pernicious is that people do not recognize that they are being affected, somehow, by the metaphors they hear and often adopt as models for their behavior. That is, people who listen to a song such as "All in the Game" do not recognize that their ideas have been influenced, in any way, by the song. In the same way, we do not realize the degree to which our consciousness has been affected by metaphors and other ideas found in songs and other forms of popular culture. (As a footnote to this, let me point out that the incredible popularity of *Survivor* shows the significance of games in American culture. The show was looked on as a game and the winner was the person who played the game the best.)

## ON THE POWER OF IDENTIFICATION WITH SYMBOLIC HEROES, HEROINES, AND CELEBRITIES

When we are young, it is quite natural to identify with symbolic heroes and heroines (and perhaps also celebrities) with whom we come in contact in popular culture. These heroes and heroines, many of whom are fictional (found in stories we are read as children, comic books, television shows, films, etc.) are often strong, good looking, and generally do remarkable things and gain great admiration.

The term *identification* is generally defined as a process in which someone becomes like someone else. That is, identification involves trying to become like someone in various ways, such as trying to think or act or look like the person we identify with.

When we identify with powerful heroic figures, we "participate," so to speak, in the power and glory of these heroic figures. Thus, we derive a kind of "halo" effect from identifying with a character like Superman or Wonder Woman. A weak and relatively powerless child escapes from this status by identifying with Superman or some other hero or heroine. Some of these heroes and heroines may be sports figures—wonderful baseball players, football players, basketball players, tennis players, and lately, golfers like Tiger Woods.

I discovered, when giving a lecture tour of the Scandinavian countries a few years ago, that the young son of one of the professors I was visiting knew the names of all the "superstar" pro basketball players. As we develop, and go through various stages in our lives, these heroic figures with whom we identify, may change considerably—depending on our stage of development at the time. This process of identification is something we are not generally conscious of, even though it is very important to us. Ultimately, it helps us liberate ourselves from the domination of our parents, and in particular our mothers. But young children don't know what the concept *identification* means. They do, however, know how to identify with heroes and heroines.

As Joseph Henderson explains in "Ancient Myths and Modern Man" (cited in Jung, 1968), we use our identification with heroic figures to liberate ourselves from infantile desires, such as wanting to stay a child and be taken care of by our mothers. What Henderson pointed out is that heroes and heroines of all kinds help us separate ourselves from our mothers and parents and enable us to become individuals and grow up.

This process of identification with heroic figures (male and female as well as animals, etc.) from popular culture is of considerable importance to us and not, by any means, a trivial matter. At a very early age, now, many young children in America spend hours watching television programs with heroic figures; in addition, we read stories to our children, and they learn about other heroic figures in nursery school and kindergarten.

Thus, it is reasonable to suggest that popular culture plays an important role in socializing Americans (and those in other cultures as well) from a very early age. Unfortunately, not all the socialization done by popular culture is good for children; in fact, one might argue just the opposite. Unfortunately, what children learn from television, video games, films, and other popular culture and media all too often tends to be quite destructive of their well-being.

## MIMESIS OR IMITATION

*Mimesis* is the Latin term for "imitation," which is one of the more important theories of art. In his *Poetics*, Aristotle suggested that the arts are based on imitation. He wrote, "Epic poetry and Tragedy, Comedy also and Dithyrambic poetry, and the music of the flute and of the lyre in most of their forms are all in their general conception modes of imitation." If art is an imitation of life, this gives it a lower status than life itself.

M. H. Abrams (1958), a literary theorist, wrote an influential book, *The Mirror and the Lamp: Romantic Theory and the Critical Tradition,* which offers four fundamental critical orientations, including mimesis. These are:

1. Mimetic Theories of Art. In Abrams' typology, those who believe in "mimetic" theories of art suggest it is a "mirror."

2. **Objective Theories of Art.** These theorists argue that rather than imitating reality like a mirror, art projects its own more-or-less self-contained reality. It is thus opposed to the mirror and is represented by the "lamp." As Abrams suggested, this orientation regards texts isolated from other considerations, as self-sufficient entities, which are to be evaluated on the basis of their internal relations. We are close to the notion that art exists only for art's sake.
3. **Pragmatic Theories of Art.** These theories suggest that art is functional, that it does things, such as teaching us about life, instilling moral values in people, persuading us to do certain things, and so on. Advertising would be a good example of a pragmatic use of art, and so is propaganda. The focus is on how art can be used to accomplish certain things.
4. **Expressive Theories of Art.** These theories focus on the creators of works of art and the creative processes, along with the emotional kicks that works of art generate in people.

Although Abrams wrote about literature and theories that focused on literature, we can extend the range and use these four theories to analyze the mass media and interpret the texts carried by the media. We can also see that many of the theories of art developed in recent years can be traced back to these four basic theories. For example, it can be suggested that auteur theory, which focuses on the role of the director in film-making, is essentially an expressive theory of art.

Abrams also offered an analysis that, he suggested, shows how these theories relate to one another in an over-arching framework. We find an artist and an audience at the lowest level of his schema. Above them we find the work of art and above that the universe. Because Abrams was dealing with literature and printed texts, he did not include media in his formulations. I suggest there are five focal points we might consider:

1. The *art work* or text.
2. *America or the society* in which the art work is found.
3. The *medium* the art work uses.
4. The *audience* for the art work.
5. The *artist* (or creative team) that creates the text.

These focal points enable us to discuss texts in terms of their creators, the media that carry them, their audiences, and society at large. I have used alliteration here as a mnemonic device. Every element can be connected, either directly or indirectly, with every other element in this list of focal points.

## MIMETIC DESIRE

With mimetic desire, we take the notion of imitation a step further. We are familiar with the notion that mimesis involves imitation from the words *mime* and *mimic*. Mimes are performers who imitate certain activities without saying anything to explain what they are doing. And mimics imitate—so as to ridicule, generally—someone's speech, body language.

According to the French critic René Girard (1991), who developed the concept and explained its importance in his book *A Theater of Envy*, mimetic desire plays an important role in our lives. Girard argued that although we can understand the role of mimicry in matters such as fashion, facial expression, and the arts, we seldom think about it as it as involving desire and seldom recognize that it may be affecting us.

Girard suggested that imitation is actually a powerful social force involved in everything from human gregariousness to conformity. Imitation has a double valence: It both draws us together and pulls us apart, and frequently does this at the same time. When we can share something we desire, we are united, but when we cannot, we become enemies.

Girard's book is about Shakespeare's plays. Girard argued that the basic force motivating the characters in Shakespeare is mimetic desire; it is, he suggested, the key to understanding Shakespeare, and *A Theater of Envy* examines Shakespeare's plays and shows how mimetic desire informs and pervades them.

Remember, mimetic desire means that people desire objects not for their intrinsic or essential value but, in essence, because someone else desires them; we imitate the desire of others in mimetic desire. Thus, as Girard explained, in the story of Helen of Troy the Greeks want Helen back because the Trojans don't want to give her up and the Trojans don't want to give her up because the Greeks want her. Mimetic circles, he suggested, are vicious circles.

We have to make a distinction between mimetic desire and envy. Envy is always mimetic but not all mimetic desire is based on envy. That is because, as Girard sees things, mimetic desire is so complex and assumes so many different forms that to say it is the same thing as envy is too reductionistic.

It is possible, Girard suggested, to see mimetic desire as functioning in advertising. Audiences of television commercials and print advertisements are premised on our desiring what those we see in advertising desire—that is, on our identifying with and imitating the desire of the actors and actresses—and in many case celebrities— in advertising. That is, the underlying reason, Girard claimed, behind our purchasing Levi's jeans or Fidji perfume or whatever is that we imitate the desire of those we see using these products.

## MODELS WE IMITATE

I make a distinction between heroes and models. Heroes and heroines are persons who achieve great things and are recognized for their achievements. Models, on the other hands, are people whose looks and behavior (and this includes everything from fashions to use of language to taste in foods and drinks) we imitate—often consciously but sometimes unconsciously. Models may be decidedly unheroic, and may even be evil. Villains are often more attractive and interesting, alas, than decent or ordinary and sometimes even more heroic figures.

If we cannot imitate their actions, we can—and often do— imitate the clothes our models wear, the drinks they consume, the foods they eat, the fashion statements they make (such as earrings, eyeglass styles, body language, speech mannerisms, and the way they relate to members of the opposite sex). We may start with our parents or teachers and move on to characters from films, television, music videos (God forbid) and other works of popular culture.

Many adolescents, for example, take rock musicians as their models and thus adopt the "look" of various musicians, some of whom do not lead exemplary lives, it should be said. For a while, a few years ago, the so-called "grunge" look was popular, due to the popularity of various grunge bands. As new bands with new looks become popular, millions of young men and women, generally in their adolescent years, adopt the look of the members of these bands.

## THE POWER OF IMAGES AND STYLE

What an image is actually is rather complicated. We know that the term is connected with the idea of some kind of visual presentation or representation. In semiotic parlance (semiotics being the science of signs), an image can be thought of as a collection of signs. A sign can be understood as anything that can be used to stand for something else. One of the founding fathers of semiotics, Saussure, suggested that signs have two components: a sound or image aspect, which he called a *signifier,* and a concept tied to the sound or image, which he called a *signified.* The relation between a signifier and a signified is based on convention; that is, it is arbitrary.

When people talk about their "images" they really mean the ideas and associations generated by the way they look, primarily, and act. The way they look would be the signifiers they put together (clothes, hairstyles, body adornments, kinds of glasses, etc.) and the image represents the notions, concepts, ideas or signifieds, semiotically speaking, that people get from their look. What we call "people reading," trying to figure out what people are like when we look at them, is really a matter, from a semiotic perspective, of making sense of or "reading" their signifiers. We read these signifiers so quickly and are so adept at doing so, and so we do not think, very much, about the process they are involved with. When we look at a photograph, for example, we "read" the photograph in terms of its signifiers, and the same can be said for each moment in a film or television program.

Sometimes, images have an immediate, powerful, visceral impact—based on the nature of the lighting and other aesthetic matters. A few years ago in a children's program in Japan, there was an image involving a very bright light that traumatized a large number of viewers and had a considerable neurological and psychological impact, for an extended period of time. It sent hundreds of people to the hospital and later sent millions of kids scurrying to buy the Pokémon characters in card packs. So images can have all kinds of effects, from giving us a sense of what a person is like (in one sense of the term) to generating physiological effects of a rather profound nature.

## THE POWER OF INFORMATION

Information, although we may not think of it as such, often has a controlling (or perhaps, at times, even coercive) power. If we think that X brand of car is more reliable and cheaper to operate than other brands, that bit of information may determine what kind of car we buy. It may not, of course—we may be swayed by our desire for status or by the looks of a car that is not safe and not reliable. If we find out that our lover is cheating on us, that will affect—rather profoundly, one might imagine—our relationship.

In *Genesis,* it was when Adam and Eve ate from the Tree of Knowledge that their eyes were opened and they recognized that they were naked. When God found out that they had disobeyed him, he threw them out of the Garden of Eden. This story shows the power of information. The story of Adam and Eve, of course, has had an enormous impact on Western philosophical and religious thought as well as institutions. Let me quote the famous lines: "The Lord God took the man and placed him in the Garden of Eden, to till it and tend it. And the Lord God commanded the man saying 'Of every tree of the garden you are free to eat; but as for the tree of knowledge of good and bad, you must not eat of it; for as soon as you eat of it, you shall die.'" Shortly after that, the serpent tempted Eve, who convinced Adam to eat from the tree, as she had done, and that led to Adam and Eve being expelled from the Garden of Eden and all kinds of dire consequences for men, women and snakes.

We also consider that having certain information and failing to act on the basis of this information is often immoral. Thus, in a celebrated murder case that occurred in Berkeley recently, a young college student who did nothing when he saw his best friend drag a young girl into a bathroom, where he later raped and killed her, has been condemned for not doing anything to save the girl's life. Not doing something, in certain situations, we must recognize, is a form of action.

## THE POWER OF STORIES

Most of the texts we are involved with in our daily experiences of popular culture are narratives—stories about individuals and groups that usually involve conflicts and resolutions. Most of the genres we find in our everyday lives and in the mass media are narratives— whether it be conversations, fairy tales, myths, children's stories, fables, commercials, sitcoms, soap operas, detective novels, reality shows like *Survivor,* and so on. Because we are exposed to hundreds of commercials in a given day, we tend to forget or not notice that we are watching narratives. But they have a power over us, in that we see models to imitate and gain insights into the effects of people's behavior.

As Michel de Certeau (1984) explained in *The Practice of Everyday Life,* we are continually being bombarded by narrations of one sort or another. They are found in journalism, advertising, television programs, and pervade our media. We are always being told stories and events are always being turned into stories by the media. Certeau's point is very important: We swim, like fish, in a sea of stories and these stories have the power to shape our ideas and our behavior. These stories are what transmit our culture and give us our culture, or, in technical terms, enculturate us.

As we develop intellectually and emotionally, the kinds of stories we read, hear, and are told become increasingly more complex. Thus, we are read children's stories and fairy tales when we are young, and when we are old, we are able to read sophisticated and complex novels. At each stage in our development, there are stories that are available to us and that are appropriate to us. (There are, of course, others that are accessible to us but not appropriate to our level of development, which creates many problems.) And these stories all do a variety of things—they entertain us, they reflect our beliefs and values, they reinforce some values and neglect others. In short, they teach us, at all times, even though we may not be aware that this is what is happening.

Let me offer an example of the way in which narratives reflect ideas and stereotypes. I will do this by dealing with a very short form of narratives—jokes.

## Jokes as Narratives

Jokes are narratives, we must recall. They can be defined as short humorous stories, meant to amuse, with punch lines. In this section, I deal with a joke about the aged and sexuality. Here, we have humor dealing with matters of considerable importance to people. Humor is a precious gift, one of the few things that we like that is also good for us. The average person laughs more than a dozen times a day (according to figures in the *Harper's Index*) and this laughter serves a number of functions. Happy or mirthful laughter is, strange as it may seem, a mild form of exercise that activates our muscles, increases our heart rate, and reduces stress. After we laugh, we relax physically for a brief period and this helps diminish tension and anger.

Laughter makes us happy and less self-conscious as we hear jokes about the absurd things people do and speculate about how foolish people (including ourselves) often are. Our jokes, which are probably the most popular form of oral humor, often make fun of powerful people and institutions and help liberate us from rigid thinking and obsessive beliefs.

Humor, then, is a force that helps us resist the daily pressures we experience and helps us better accommodate ourselves to the world. The greatest humorists are close to being anarchists; they don't seem to respect anyone or anything and often blast through the boundaries of good taste or conventional thinking. By doing this humorists help liberate us from anxieties and being bound by conventions.

But humor also often has an aggressive aspect to it and in certain situations can be a coercive or directive force. In small groups, humor can push people to think or behave in certain ways—those favored by the person making the jokes and using humor to accomplish certain tasks. A look at the monologues of the great comedians on the late evening shows demonstrates this combination of aggression and coercion; a lot of people—politicians, performers, celebrities, and groups of one sort or another—came in for some biting ridicule. We see the same thing in cartoons in *The New Yorker* that make fun of various kinds of people and the "insulting" greeting cards that have become very popular recently. The message is—escape ridicule by conforming to commonly accepted kinds of behavior.

There is still another aspect of humor that should be mentioned here, another thing that humor does for us. Humor also often reveals hidden attitudes and unrecognized beliefs that people have, and thus jokes are a useful tool for finding out what's going on in society. A good example of how humor attacks, coerces, and reveals hidden notions is found in jokes about sexuality and the aged.

When we look at sex jokes about aged people we tend to find two dominant stereotypes: men who are "too old to cut the mustard anymore" and "sex-starved" older women. These jokes and others about aged people are an insidious force that oppress their targets by ridiculing them, by insulting them, and by giving them ugly and inaccurate images of themselves. What is disturbing about all this is that humor is conventionally seen as harmless entertainment. Because our humorists are privileged and untouchable, victimized individuals and groups find it difficult to fight back against the stereotypes and images that humorists make popular.

Let me show this by taking a fascinating and complicated joke about sexuality and the aged and showing what it reflects about conventional attitudes on this matter. The joke is "cute" and seemingly harmless, but it spreads a notion about the sexuality of the aged that is quite pernicious. This joke, and jokes like it, reinforce notions many people have about the sexual behavior of men and women in their 70s, 80s, and 90s—namely that these people do not and cannot have sex lives. I call this joke "The Tan."

> *A man goes to Miami Beach for a vacation. After a few days on the beach he looks in the mirror and notices that he has a gorgeous brown tan all over his body except for his penis. He decides to remedy the situation. The next day he gets up early in the morning, walks to a deserted section of the beach, takes off his clothes and lies down. He starts putting sand all over his body until only his penis is exposed to the sun. A short while later a couple of little old ladies walk by. One*

> *notices the penis sticking up in the sand. She points it out to her friend. "When I was 20," she says, "I was scared to death of them. When I was 40, I couldn't get enough of them. When I was 60, I couldn't get one to come near me* . . . **And now they're growing wild on the beach!"**

I don't tell jokes very well, but when I tell this joke to people, they always find it very amusing. Why might this be?

The most immediate thing we notice about the joke is its sexual content. It is not a "dirty" joke, but it is about people's sexuality and that is a subject that people find absorbing, because we are all sexual beings—in addition to whatever else we might be. And we all have a lot of anxiety about our sexuality. The joke deals with the sexual development of the woman telling the joke, as she passes from 20 to 40 to 60, and by implication, the joke deals with the sexuality of women in general. That is, it offers and reinforces conventional notions about women's sexuality, suggesting that they all pass through three stages: fear of sex when young, insatiable desire for sex when middle aged, and lack of sex when aged.

When the woman was 60, remember, she "couldn't get one to come near me" because, we are led to assume, aged women are not attractive or desirable. (At what point, we might ask, does a woman become less beautiful and less desirable, and to whom?) This notion about the sexuality of aged women and men is quite absurd, but it is widely held and it is reinforced by jokes like "The Tan." Because it is widely held, it serves to give older men and women a false picture of how they should behave—basically desexualizing them. This image can contribute to aged people giving up on the sexual part of their lives since people tend to act the way they think they are supposed to act.

Ironically, the punch line of the joke represents a kind of paradisiacal state in which penises grow wild on the beach and thus are easily obtainable by everyone in as great a quantity as might be desired. Sexual repression, which Freud postulated as being the price we all pay for civilization, is no longer a significant force.

The man in the joke, it could be argued, has unconscious exhibitionist tendencies that are masked by his alleged desire or perhaps even fixation about obtaining an even tan on every part of his body. There may also be an element of narcissism in wanting a "perfect" tan. And this joke also suggests that the woman who recounts her sexual history has regressed to a state in which she either does not know or has forgotten that penises always come connected to a man. They never grow wild at the beach—or any other place.

Jokes actually are much more complicated than they seem. Technically they are stories people tell, meant to amuse, that have a punch line. This punch line, which surprises us, generates the laughter. If this element of surprise is missing, as in jokes that we've already heard, we no longer find the jokes funny. We make sense of jokes by unconsciously setting up in our minds various oppositional relationships. In "The Tan," for example, there is an opposition between the beach (i.e., the world of nature) and society, between free sexuality and repression, and between different attitudes toward sex at 20, 40, and 60, and what we might call "growing wild" sex that is abundant and easily obtainable by all.

The joke involves what might be described as private parts in public places and deals with two characters, each of whom is deficient in some respect. The man who is so driven about his tan is foolish; people don't get tans over every inch of their bodies, or if they wish to do so, they tan themselves in private places where others will not observe their genitals. The woman who sees the man's private parts is mistaken, assuming or hoping, presumably because she is so sex-starved, that they are now growing wild on the beach.

According to popular stereotypes, "little old ladies" and aged men aren't supposed to be interested in sex, aren't capable of having sex or are sex-starved and find sex unobtainable. That is the absurd notion fostered by jokes like "The Tan" and many other jokes about sexuality and the aged. These jokes are populated by sexually undesirable and therefore sex-starved aged women (who haven't yet "renounced" their sexual lives) and aged men who are incapable of performing sexually.

Our attitudes about sexuality and the aged lead me to suggest that these jokes really deal with unconscious and repressed anxieties young and middle-aged people have about their sexual lives when they grow older. They are probably afraid that they will not be able to enjoy sex then. So they desexualize the aged. By doing this they diminish the sense of loss they fear they will feel.

But when men and women are aged, unless they have suffered very serious illnesses or been completely brainwashed by ridiculous jokes about sexuality and the aged, they will still be able to find sex pleasurable. Scientific reports show that men and women in their 90s are still capable of having orgasms so we're never too old, it seems, to have sexual lives and to enjoy sex. The joke, then, is really on the people who tell jokes ridiculing the idea that aged people can have sex lives. When they become aged, they might not find a joke like "The Tan" so funny!

## THE POWER OF SPECTACLES: THE SUPER BOWL

One of the ways people become tied more strongly to their social groups, subcultures, and cultures is through participation in spectacles such as parades, celebrations, attending football games (or watching them on television), and similar kinds of activities. These spectacles entertain us, but they also reinforce our connection with American culture and society and its values and beliefs. People in large groups have a different sense of themselves and often behave differently than they do when alone.

As the great sociologist Gustave Le Bon (1960) explained in his classic work, *The Crowd,* people in crowds, whatever their level of education, intelligence, or character become part of some kind of a collective mind that makes them think, feel, and behave quite differently from the way they would behave on their own, as individuals. At football games, for example, when you are in a stadium with 70,000 or 100,000 fans, you can feel a remarkable sense of excitement and anticipation—and anxiety—as the game progresses. Spectacles are an important genre in television, which I deal with in more detail in my chapter on the Super Bowl.

## HOW CONCEPTS ARE DEFINED AND HOW THEY AFFECT US

I conclude this chapter with a discussion of how concepts are defined and how they affect us. When we watch a football game or a film or a television program or read a spy story or a mystery or participate in popular culture, one way or another, behind the actions of the characters we can usually find some theme or idea or belief that is connected to them or helps explain them. And sometimes, to help us, a character in a story, will explain his or her behavior for us and spell it out in terms of ideas, principles, rules, codes, whatever. These are all, as I understand things, concepts.

What is remarkable about concepts is that we make sense of them in a rather convoluted way—we define them in terms of their not being their opposites. This point was made by the great Swiss linguist Ferdinand de Saussure (1966), who wrote, "Concepts are purely differential and defined not by their positive content but negatively by their relations with the other terms of the system" (p. 117).

And, as he added, the "most precise characteristic" of these concepts "is in being what others are not." What Saussure was arguing is that we make sense of things in terms of their relations with other terms; in other words, nothing has meaning in itself.

We are always, although we may not be aware of what we are doing, making sense of concepts (as well as characters in stories and their actions) by establishing, in our minds, sets of polar oppositions: win, lose; exciting, dull; happy, sad; poor, rich; hero, villain . . . and on and on it goes. We make these oppositions because of the nature of language, Saussure argued. He was not saying that everything in life should be seen in terms of black and white but that when it comes to concepts, ideas (and I add characters), we are forced, by language, to see relationships and the most important one is oppositions.

When we watch football games (which, I argue, can be seen as narratives or narrative-like) or sitcoms or soaps or spy stories, and so on, we are always "reading" what characters say and do in terms of concepts like hero, villain; good girl, temptress; great guy, jerk. Thus, language compels us to search for meaning in terms of relationships and oppositions.

## THE POWER OF MUSIC

My last topic involves the power of music to generate strong emotions and feelings. In my analysis of the song "It's All in the Game" I dealt with what might be described as cultural imperatives in the metaphors found in the song's lyrics. But in addition to the lyrics of a song, which by using rhyme, can have a considerable amount of power, there is also the matter of the melody of the song (or of music, in general) and the beat—especially in rock music, Latin music, and so on.

It is difficult to say why music can generate strong emotional responses. In the case of popular song, we must remember that we have the power of narratives at work, also. These songs tell stories about people that mean something to us. At the gym where I work out, all the songs seem to be about some aspect of "love" or of feelings created by lost love, new love, what you will. So the stories in songs can move us. But there is more to a song than a story; there is also the melody and the beat. In some songs, the lyrics seem rather stupid if you look at them in their printed form; it is only when you hear the song, and see how the lyrics relate to the melody and the beat, that the song makes sense.

As James Lull (1992) explained in his book *Popular Music and Communication*, popular music has a remarkable ability to affect the consciousness of people who hear this music through such techniques as the power of thematic repetition and "hooks" that repeatedly use melodies and rhythms to grab onto the attention of listeners. These songs are played over and over again on radio stations when they first appear and after a number of years as "oldies," which means their power to affect listeners is even more greatly enhanced.

We see, then, that because of a variety of factors—repetition, the catchy nature of the hook, the lyrics, and the beat—music (and especially popular music) has a uniquely powerful hold on many people. I can recall that after a week at my gym, where Paula Cole's "Where Have all the Cowboy's Gone" was played over and over again, I started wondering where they had gone myself. I should point out that I listen to classical music all the time and, even though it is generally without lyrics, classical music has a remarkable power to stir my emotions. And, as anyone who has ever attended a rock concert or a classical music concert can attest, music profoundly affects the emotions of audiences who attend these concerts.

Allan Bloom (1983), a conservative critic of American culture, described the influence of rock music on American youth in very negative terms. He argued that rock music and rock culture (and now, perhaps, we can add hip-hop) has become the most important influence on children between 12 and 18, displacing the church, parents, and the school. The heroes of rock music, he suggested, are drug-ridden, sex-crazy "guttersnipes" whose songs debase those who listen to them. He considered this music to be "junk food." He wrote:

> One thing I have no difficulty teaching students today is the passage in the *Republic* where Socrates explains that control over music is control over character and that the rhythm and the melody are more powerful than the words. They do not especially like Socrates's views on music, but they understand perfectly what he is about and the importance of the issue.

You may not agree with Bloom's assessment of rock music but his point, taken from Socrates, about its power and influence and of the importance of rhythm and melody is hard to argue with—especially since the words in many rock music songs are hard to hear and understand. I would suggest, however, that in many cases, the words to songs are also important and have a powerful effect on listeners.

We also can see the power of music at work in religious services, in which songs play an important role in giving people a sense of community and a sense of the divine. In some cases, people sing songs in Latin or Hebrew and don't necessarily know the meaning of the words they are singing. But the melodies are so beautiful (many of the Hebrew songs happen to be in a minor key, and minor keys seem to have a remarkable power to stir the emotions), that people derive a great sense of pleasure and satisfaction from singing these songs.

## CONCLUSIONS

In this chapter I have suggested that popular culture and the mass media that carry various forms or kinds of popular culture are not simple entertainments that wash off our minds and consciousness the way water washes off a duck's back. We are, more than we may imagine, profoundly affected by popular culture, which has now, in many cases, become a more dominant socializing influence on us than our parents.

What we must do is learn how to interpret popular culture and learn how to understand its power, so we can cope with it, so we can make rational and intelligent decisions about our behavior. There are, I am suggesting, all kinds of unconscious imperatives and effects from popular culture that we must learn how to recognize and deal with. If we don't, we may go through life believing "love is a game" and all kinds of other ridiculous and frequently self-destructive things.

Chapter 3

# The Power of Groups

We saw, in the last chapter, that what individuals do and what they think is, to a considerable degree, affected by accidents of birth. By accidents of birth I mean things such as the family they are born into, the country they live in, the language they hear and learn to speak (or languages), their race, religion, intelligence, personality, and so on. In this chapter I deal more directly with the way groups shape our consciousness and, in particular, our taste. It isn't a simple matter of groups being able to control us—except, perhaps in cults and similar organizations—but there is no question, I would say, that societies, working through institutions do exert various degrees of control on their members. That's what social psychology is all about.

In this chapter, I discuss the following topics related to the influence of groups on popular culture and social and political matters:

1. Political cultures (and the theories of Aaron Wildavsky).
2. Taste cultures (and the theories of Herbert J. Gans).
3. The significance of postmodernism.

The aim of this chapter is to suggest the degree to which our taste in popular culture and media is tied to societal, political, and cultural considerations. We are individuals with distinctive personality traits and characteristics but we are, as I suggested earlier, also social animals and are profoundly affected by accidents of birth such as race, religion, ethnicity, gender, and the socioeconomic class of our parents.

## POLITICAL CULTURES

One of the most interesting efforts at understanding how groups—in this case political cultures—may shape our behavior was done by the late political scientist, Aaron Wildavsky. He was a professor of political science at the University of California and the author of numerous books and articles. In the later stages of his career he became interested in cultural theory. He argued, and I'm slightly simplifying his notions, that in every democratic society there are four political cultures—people who have certain notions about politics. These four political cultures are, in his terms: individualists, elitists, egalitarians, and fatalists. I discuss these terms shortly.

How did Wildavsky arrive at this grouping of four political cultures? He discussed the basic problems of cultural theory as follows. The dimensions of cultural theory, he argued, are based on answers to two questions: the first involves our identities and asks "Who am I?" The second involves our actions and asks "How should I behave?" He answers the question of identity (Who am I?) by suggesting that individuals belong either to a strong group or a weak group. A strong group is one that that makes decisions that are binding on all members, whereas in a weak group people have weak ties to others and their choices only affect and are binding on themselves. When it comes to action (How should I behave?), we find that individuals are subject to either many or few prescriptions or rules. That is, we have either "free spirits" or people who are tightly constrained.

Wildavsky suggested, then, that we can belong to groups that exercise tight control over us or groups that are rather weak and that allow us to make most of our own decisions. And when it comes to actions, we find ourselves able to do more or less whatever we want or constrained by numerous rules and regulations.

Thus, we have two basic matters to consider: groups (which can be weak or strong) and rules or prescriptions (which can be numerous and varied or few in number). From these two considerations Wildavsky said we get our four political cultures:

**Elitists:**     strong group, many prescriptions.
**Egalitarians:** strong group, few prescriptions.

**Fatalists:** weak group, many prescriptions.
**Individualists:** weak group, few prescriptions.

Elitists, who believe that hierarchy is necessary for the good of society (and are fortunate to have fatalists to lord over, so to speak) are in groups that have strong boundaries and numerous and varied prescriptions. Egalitarians, who seek to raise up the poor, downtrodden fatalists (and who stress equality of needs in people) are also in strong groups, but these groups have few rules and prescriptions. Fatalists are in weak groups but because they are, to a considerable degree, controlled by others, they have to endure many prescriptions. Individualists, mostly in the form of small businessmen who want the government to defend the country against invasion and criminals (and not do very much more) are in weak groups and have few prescriptions.

Wildavsky discussed how he developed his notion of the four groupings and how they are related to one another. Strong groups, he suggested, are those with many prescriptions that differ with social roles. They lead to elites. But strong groups whose members accept few prescriptions lead to egalitarians, a life based in great measure on voluntary consent. When you find few prescriptions and weak boundaries, you get individualists, who form new combinations and groups with ease. When you find many prescriptions and weak boundaries you get fatalists, who find that their decisions are made by others and have little power to change their situation.

What is important to remember here is that the various groups need each other and that membership in groups is generally fluid (except for fatalists): People can move from one group to another. For example, a person can be an individualist and become an egalitarian (or vice versa) depending on circumstances. A former neighbor of mine was a pilot and was a strong individualist, but when the airline that he worked for started making him do things he didn't want to do, and treating him poorly, he became an egalitarian and joined a union. It's not unusual for people to change their ideas about politics as they get older and move from one political culture to another.

What this means is that a person's choice in music may indicate either of two things: that he or she is a member of the group whose values are reflected in that music or that the person is in the process of moving to that political culture or contemplating a move to that political culture. A person who likes "My Way" can be either an individualist who wants the freedom to do as he or she chooses or, for example, an egalitarian who may be thinking about changing his or her values and beliefs to individualism. So the choices people make cannot always identify them with any degree of certainty as members of one political culture or another.

Let me point out that people in the general public do not identify themselves as being members of these political cultures. What Wildavsky argued is that people with certain beliefs can be seen, by researchers and scholars, as being members of one of the four political cultures, based on the beliefs these people have about things like risk, leadership, envy, and various other matters. Wildavsky, as a political scientist, was interested in how membership in a political culture affected political beliefs and voting. He suggested that the elitists (whose beliefs generate order) and the individualists (whose activities generate economic growth) formed the establishment in societies and that the egalitarians functioned, generally, as critics of the establishment. The fatalists, for all practical purposes, played a minor role in things and were more or less outside of the political realm—since they exercised little control over their lives.

But his political cultures also have significance for the study of popular culture, because we can consider these four political cultures as kinds of audiences for popular culture and the media, whose values and beliefs may shape, in certain ways, their choices of television programs, films, and so on.

My notion that these political cultures function as taste cultures or discrete audiences for popular culture is based on two considerations. First, there is the matter of *cognitive dissonance*. Cognitive dissonance can be understood as feelings of being disturbed or uncomfortable that are generated by exposure to ideas that conflict with one's basic values and beliefs. Thus, people tend to avoid popular culture that has content that conflicts with their belief system. Thus, elitists would tend, unconsciously I argue, to look for television programs that support their elitist views of life (that hierarchy is necessary and good for society) and avoid programs that challenge their beliefs. For example, a song like "God Save the Queen" has hierarchical and elitist values and would be congruent with the value of elitists. A song like "My Way" is not elitist in its value system but individualistic; in principle, neither elitists nor egalitarians would like "My Way." Or, to be more precise, should like it, if they thought about the values found in "My Way."

Second, there is the matter, just alluded to, of *reinforcement*. We tend to look for popular culture texts that support our beliefs and make us feel good about these beliefs. This is reinforcement. Thus, we tend to choose films, television shows, and music, on the basis of avoiding dissonance and reinforcing the beliefs that we have.

Egalitarians would prefer songs like "We Are The World" that have an egalitarian value system to them, but individualists wouldn't like such songs.

## TASTE CULTURES

The distinguished sociologist Herbert J. Gans (1974) wrote a book a number of years ago, *Popular Culture and High Culture*, which offers some interesting insights into the relationship between popular culture and high (or what we have called "elite") culture. Gans argued that critics have greatly exaggerated the differences between popular culture and high (or elite) culture and neglected their similarities. He suggested that popular culture is what he called a "taste culture" that is selected by people who don't have the economic backgrounds and advantages of people who like high culture. Gans added that in America there are numerous taste cultures, each of which has its own aesthetic standards for music, art, literature, and other arts.

Gans pointed out that taste cultures are class-based, in essence, so popular culture is as valid for those at the bottom rungs of society, who lack higher education generally speaking, as elite culture is for well-educated people. Gans' position is quite unusual and, in Wildavsky's terms, decidedly egalitarian.

Most scholars who deal with popular culture, especially scholars from the humanities, are very negative about popular culture both in terms of its aesthetic qualities and its alleged impact on people and society. In recent years, with the influence of postmodern thought, differences between elite and popular culture have been seen as minimal, but in 1974, when Gans wrote his book, his acceptance of popular culture was quite radical. As he mentioned in his book, popular culture was not thought of as a fit subject for study by sociologists in the 1970s.

I must confess that I understand what Gans is talking about. I wrote my doctoral dissertation on a satirical and widely read (at the time) comic strip, *Li'l Abner*, in 1963. My subject was considered by some professors at the University of Minnesota, where I got my degree, as scandalous and unworthy of scholarly attention.

Taste cultures are similar to political cultures in that they are what Gans called "analytic aggregates" that researchers use to categorize people as contrasted to what he called "real aggregates" whose members are conscious of their identities as members of some group or entity. But political cultures do have coherent and systematic value systems. Gans suggested that we can also find a cohesive value system in taste cultures, which tend to be random aggregates of people with similar tastes in some form of music or art or entertainment. These aggregates are also, Gans argued, created by social researchers. In keeping with his sociological perspective, Gans discussed the factors that affect people's membership in his taste cultures. These factors are matters such as socioeconomic class, age, ethnic and racial background, religion, regional origin, and place of residence along with various personality factors. He suggested that as American society becomes more homogenized, the crucial differences tend to become those based on age and class.

Gans added that class differences are based, primarily, on education—which he defined broadly, to include both schooling and what people learn from the mass media and other sources, including the family. Thus, taste cultures tend to approximate socioeconomic classes. This led Gans to suggest that there are five taste cultures:

1. High culture. High culture is that of creators of literature and the arts and critics. It is the culture of "serious" writers, artists, and members of the societal "elites." There is much concern with aesthetic issues.
2. Upper middle culture. This is made up of professionals, executives, and their wives, who have attended the "better" colleges and universities. They are drawn, Gans said, to novels that focus on individual achievement and upward mobility.
3. Lower middle culture. America's dominant taste culture made up of middle- and lower middle-class people who like works that reflect the basic values of the society: "upholding tradition and maintaining order against irrepressible sexual impulses and other upsetting influences."
4. Low culture. The culture of the lower middle classes, but mostly of factory workers and service workers and semi-skilled white-collar workers. This culture was dominant in America until the 1950s when it was replaced by lower middle-class culture. People in this taste culture are high school dropouts. They reject elite culture as effete and snobbish.
5. Quasi-folk low culture. This taste culture blends folk culture and pop culture of the pre-World War II era. It is made up of unskilled blue-collar workers, people in service jobs, and people without even a high school education.

They read tabloids and comic books, watch Mexican soap operas (for the Spanish-speaking members of this taste culture), and consume other materials generally seen as junk.

American sociologists and social commentators have been ingenious in making lists of different social and cultural groups found in America. There are numerous classification systems that have been made, some by satirists and writers, others by serious scholars: highbrow, middlebrow, lowbrow, U and non-U, and so on.

There is a slight similarity between Wildavsky's political cultures and Gans' taste cultures. Wildavsky's elitists are similar to Gans's high culture people; Wildavsky's individualists are similar to those Gans said like upper middle culture; and Wildavsky's fatalists are similar to those Gans said are attracted to low culture and quasi-folk culture. Egalitarians don't fit into this schema. The problem is that egalitarians are often wealthy and sophisticated individuals whose culture is closer to high culture than the "low" culture of the people the egalitarians are trying to help, the fatalists. Egalitarians have certain values and beliefs but their culture, in Gans' terms, can be anything but fatalist, I would suggest.

It is worth considering some of the examples Gans gave for each taste culture. He admitted, in his book, that he was only giving very broad approximations; nevertheless, it is interesting to see what—according to Gans, writing 30 years ago—each of these cultures likes.

> High culture: *Finnegan's Wake*, modern music, primitive art, abstract expressionism, chamber music.
> Upper middle culture: *Time, Newsweek, Psychology Today, Harper's, New Yorker*, 19th-century symphonic and operatic works, Broadway musicals.
> Lower middle culture: Norman Rockwell paintings, *Life, Saturday Evening Post, Reader's Digest,* Harold Robbins novels, *Bonanza, All in the Family, The Mary Tyler Moore Show.*
> Low culture: Westerns, *I Love Lucy, The Ed Sullivan Show, The Beverly Hillbillies, The Lawrence Welk Show.*
> Quasi-folk low culture: Tabloids, comic books, old westerns, Mexican soaps for Spanish speakers.

We must keep in mind that Gans published his book in 1974, and tastes and other related matters change very quickly, especially when it comes to popular culture. In popular culture, fads and crazes come and go quickly. A few years can be an eternity when dealing with popular taste, so what can be said about popular taste 30 years ago must take time considerations into account. As I write this, *Who Wants to be a Millionaire* is rapidly losing popularity and America is waiting for the next version of *Survivor*.

Of course, one can argue that the television shows and movies and other examples of popular culture for each of Gans' taste cultures have changed, but the five taste cultures have not, in part because the makeup of the socioeconomic classes in America have not changed radically. And Gans acknowledged that his taste cultures were rough approximations. He also discussed youth culture, Black culture, and ethnic cultures in his book.

Gans made an important point in his discussion of the social structure of taste publics and cultures, namely, that culture has political consequences, even though taste cultures are not explicitly political, and that is because our entertainments and mass-mediated cultures reflect and express values and deal with relationships that are implicitly political. Thus, for example, television sitcoms and family comedies deal with relationships between men and women and parents and children, and thus reflect values and matters relating to power that are in these texts, even if those who watch them do not recognize this to be the case.

## A Brief Note on Taste: *De Gustibus Non Disputandem Est*

This phrase can be translated as "there's no disputing taste," but taste is continually subject to change because of advertising, peer pressure, fads in fashion that suddenly become popular, and similar phenomena. What this means is that each person has a right to his or her own taste in whatever it is one might be talking about: choice of furniture, clothes, movies, television shows, novels, and so on. And, as Gans pointed out, each person's taste is valid for that person: It entertains him or her, it reflects the person's values and beliefs, and it provides models to imitate. Although there may not be any disputing taste, it does not mean that all taste cultures are equal in terms of the aesthetic qualities of the texts and other aspects of culture each taste culture likes. Romance novels are not equal to the novels of Joyce or Hawthorne, Melville, Faulkner, Hemingway, or any "serious" novelist. Blue-collar workers generally have blue-collar taste and that is perfectly fine.

So, we have to make a distinction between the matter of choice of popular culture and the matter of quality of popular culture and elite culture. It is possible to make distinctions, I suggest, between different texts and the choice of texts on the various media. One can watch wrestling on television or, at least some of the time, great films, serious dramas and works by Shakespeare, Arthur Miller, and other playwrights. The medium, then, offers a variety of genres or kinds of programs and people exercise their choice in what they wish to watch.

Most people, because America is predominantly a low-culture society, in Gans' terms, watch what he would call *low culture*. But every once in a while, something appeals to a large number of people that is closer to elite culture than low culture, which raises the question of why this work was able to break through the class and taste culture barriers that prevent most low taste cultures from watching more elite kinds of texts. Is it because popular taste is being raised or elite taste it being lowered? Or is it due to accidents or chance matters such as casting a famous star, who has many fans, in a role or because of very high levels of hype?

## POSTMODERNISM AND POPULAR CULTURE

In recent years, with the development of postmodern theory (some would say the triumph of postmodern theory), the notion that there are significant differences between popular and elite culture has become suspect. Postmodernism has been defined in many ways, but one of its distinctive characteristics is its attack on moral and aesthetic absolutes, which has led to the erasing of the boundary between popular and elite art and taste, and a kind of frenzied aesthetic pluralism. (Some critics have argued that American culture is not postmodern but, rather, in the latest stage of capitalism.) Anything goes, now—or so it seems.

As Mike Featherstone (1991) explained, in *Consumer Culture & Postmodernism*, postmodernism has erased the boundary between art and everyday life and dissolved the boundary between so-called high culture and popular culture. Among the features associated with postmodernism are eclecticism, pastiche, and stylistic promiscuity, irony, playfulness, and a joy in the so-called depthlessness of culture.

One of the foremost theoreticians of postmodernism, the French thinker Jean-François Lyotard (1984), wrote, in his seminal work *The Postmodern Condition: A Report on Knowledge,* that postmodernism can be defined as "incredulity toward metanarratives," which implies that our former reliance on absolutes is no longer credible.

Lyotard's point, that we do not have meta-narratives—all inclusive systems of philosophical and speculative thought that explain life to us—has been attacked by some critics who argue that postmodernism, which attacks meta-narratives, is itself a meta-narrative. That is, you can't have a theory of postmodernism or anything else without some kind of systematic thought.

Whatever the case, we can see that postmodern theory does argue that the old boundaries that we used to erect to distinguish between elite culture and mass or popular culture no longer mean anything. There is, to simplify things somewhat, just culture, and in postmodern societies people are free to choose what they like without having to have a sense that they are displaying their lack of sophistication or taste.

Lyotard made another point worth thinking about. He argued that investigators of culture, whatever their differences, agree about "the preeminence of the narrative form in the formulation of traditional knowledge" and that "narration is the quintessential form of customary knowledge, in more ways than one" (p. 19). Postmodernists may not believe that meta-narratives have any meaning, but they are very interested in narratives, stories that teach people how to act, that offer heroes and heroines to emulate, and that bestow legitimacy on social and political institutions. It is these narratives, these stories that a culture tells itself, that help form the social bond that unites people.

And, of course, it is narratives—interpreted broadly—that are the most important element in our mass-mediated popular culture. Consider television, the dominant medium in terms of the amount of time Americans spend watching it. Most television commercials are narratives (or, to be more correct, micro-narratives). Situation comedies, soap operas (contemporary versions of epics), science fiction shows, cop shows, and most of the other genres are out and out narratives or have a strong narrative component to them. Some critics argue that news shows and documentaries also can be seen as narratives.

As I explained earlier, narratives not only entertain us but also instruct us about life: what is good and what is bad; what goals are worthwhile and what goals aren't; who's a villain and who's a hero; what's good to eat, what's good to drink, how we should dress, what kind of a car or truck or sports utility vehicle we should drive . . . the list goes on, endlessly. And much of this information comes not only from commercials but from other narratives we watch and from the behavior of heroes and heroines we admire. We learn from our experiences. What critics of popular culture ask is: Who are our teachers? What are their motives? Who licenses them? Is what they are teaching us good for us and for society?

It is these questions and other similar ones that inform my analysis of mass-mediated popular culture. Popular culture is an enormously rich source of information on American culture and character and I have "mined" this source as best I could for almost 40 years.

# Part II

*Applications*

# Chapter 4

# *Speculations on a Spectacle*
## *The Super Bowl*

Let me offer an extended analysis on one of the most famous sports spectaculars, if not the most important one, the Super Bowl. I analyze the Super Bowl from a number of different perspectives and hope that they will offer some insights worth considering.

### A CONFESSION FROM AN EX- SPORTSWRITER

Let me preface these considerations by mentioning that for a couple of years, while stationed in the army in Washington DC, I wrote high school sports for *The Washington Post*. I was fired from that position for knowing how to spell bizarre (the sports editor didn't) but then taken on week by week until I escaped from the army and went to Europe to do the Grand Tour . . . with money I made from writing sports, I might add. Who knows—maybe my interest in popular culture and the media stems, in part, from that experience—and from a college job I had flipping hamburgers.

## A DEFAMILIARIZED PERSPECTIVE ON SUPER BOWL XXXII: A REPORT FROM A MARTIAN ANTHROPOLOGIST TO THE MARTIAN PUBLIC

Football can be described as a violent spectacle in which male human beings who are either of gigantic stature or who can run extremely fast or who can throw, with some degree of accuracy, a spheroid pointed at either end, or who can catch this spheroid, engage in combat with one another. This engagement takes the form of a person running with the spheroid or throwing the spheroid or catching the spheroid—popularly known as a football. There are also specialists who can kick the spheroid long distances. Those engaged in this spectacle—called players—wear bright articles of clothing with numbers and their names on them, have some form of plastic protection devices on their shoulders and their heads (known as helmets). Players with clothing that is of the same coloration are known as members of a "team."

There are also males in striped shirts—called "officials"—with devices that emit shrieking sounds when blown and brightly colored pieces of cloth, who manage the engagement and make sure that if the rules of the engagement are violated, the team with the player doing the violation is penalized. There are many obscure and arcane rules in football—too complicated to deal with in this brief report.

This engagement takes the form of the team with the spheroid having a conference, termed a "huddle," and then executing something called a "play," which takes a few seconds of time, at the most. This pattern of having long huddles and executing plays that take only a few seconds is performed over and over. It has been estimated that the spheroid is in play no more than 10 minutes during the length of the spectacle, which can last many hours. The spectacle is performed on a green rectangular field 100 yards in length, with white lines every 10 yards, and with vertical posts and a horizontal bar in between them, at either end.

The posts are in an area known as the "end zone" which is located at either end of the field. The object of the game has been described as "penetrating an end zone," preferably by players running with the spheroid or catching the spheroid. When a team does this, it is awarded six points for scoring what is called a touchdown. If it can kick the spheroid through the posts after a touchdown, the team is awarded another point. Along the sides of this field, young and nubile women, display their legs, jump up and down and execute various jerky motions in a synchronized manner.

This exhibition is divided into four quarters and two halves. In between the halves, there are various spectacles with males and females, usually in bright uniforms, playing various musical instruments; singers; and other amusements. Football is played in huge structures known as stadiums (but at certain times as bowls), that are often capable of holding as many as 100,000 human beings. These humans imbibe various alcoholic beverages or carbonated beverages or both, and emit vocalizations (groans or expressions of extreme joy) at various moments during the spectacle.

The Super Bowl is played between the teams, each of which has won its conference championship. Determining which team is the champion is a matter that is extremely complex in some cases. The Super Bowl game is broadcast to millions of people in the United States and all over the world—many of whom do not have the slightest idea of what is going on. A perusal of descriptions of recent Super Bowls in newspapers suggests that the games were not particularly interesting, with teams from the American conference scoring many fewer points than teams from the National conference.

This game, played at the end of January every year, is the source of an enormous amount of interest and the television broadcast of the game frequently obtains the largest audience of any American television program during the year. Most of the males who play this game are multi-millionaires because of the huge salaries they are paid for their service to their teams. Why so many people in America and elsewhere find the activities of these millionaires in these exhibitions of such compelling interest remains an enigma. Further research is indicated.

## LINGUISTIC ANALYSIS

The term *super* in Super Bowl suggests something out of the ordinary, something in the realm of the superlative. Does the existence of things that are "super" somehow diminish the ordinary and give it a second-rate status? Most of us are ordinary. Are our lives made petty and trivial by the existence of superheroes and superheroines? Or even by so-called "superiors"? (I say so-called because in an individualistic society like America, where authority is not considered valid, the notion of superior beings is not generally accepted. Except for the crazies, that is, who keep waiting for them to come from outer space . . . or who believe they have already been here and are walking among us.)

What is unusual about the "bowl" part of Super Bowl is that the Super Bowl moves around the country, unlike bowls in college sports, which are located in specific stadiums. Cities are awarded a Super Bowl game and are glad to have them because they can raise the price of hotel rooms to astronomical levels for the week of the Super Bowl. (Item: Hotels in San Diego—site of the 1998 Super Bowl—which were listed in the AAA California Tourbook for $45 a night charged $100 or more during the week of the Super Bowl.)

Many of the Super Bowls are given to cities like New Orleans and Miami, which can handle large crowds and which are tourist attractions in their own right. One of the things that the Super Bowl represents, then, is the synergistic combination of tourism and entertainment—two of the world's mega-industries. And the Super Bowl is a mass-mediated entertainment that has been around long enough to become part of American folklore.

The two divisions represent different sensibilities. The National Division suggests a state or a geo-political area. It differs from the American Division, which alludes directly to the United States. What are we to make of the fact that teams from the American Football Conference have traditionally been slaughtered by teams from the National Football Conference? Does this suggest the triumph of a worldview, or globalized perspective, focused on nation-states, rather than a particularistic Americanist view, is now significant in football as well as commerce? I leave that matter for economists and sports theorists to figure out.

## A MARXIST PERSPECTIVE ON THE SUPER BOWL

(I adopt the persona of a Marxist critic here and analyze the Super Bowl using Marxist concepts.) The Super Bowl is the ultimate spectacle in a society of spectacle such as the United States. It is played by alienated millionaires, mostly African Americans, who move from team to team to obtain even larger payments for their services. The concept of the team, which suggests some kind of a long-term identification with entities beyond one's own self, has now almost completely disappeared in American sports—and in most sports played in bourgeois societies. Unfortunately, the same thing can be said about the concept of community.

The winning teams from each conference often lose star players from their team and gain star players from other teams. So, professional football teams are now most accurately described as ad hoc assemblages of alienated and disgruntled millionaires who gather together for a year or so, to try to get to the Super Bowl—to make even more money and to be given a token of their supremacy—a large ring.

The alienation of the players reflects, it can be argued, the alienation of the people who watch the game, the so-called "fans," who identify with teams as a means of escaping from the sense of pettiness and irrelevance in their own non-super lives. The players, who are mostly Black, can be looked on as an exploited racial group, for despite their millions (and not all players make that much money), the owners, who are mostly if not all White, make even more money.

One of the most important functions of the Super Bowl is to deliver the largest audience for any media event to advertisers. The game itself is embedded in a much longer multihour spectacle of analysis and discussion, during which time a huge number of television commercials are broadcast. The commercials broadcast during the Super Bowl are, cynics might say, often more entertaining than the game itself.

The Super Bowl is also connected to the real estate market and to the matter of stadium building in cities. Owners of professional football teams threaten cities with abandoning them for other cities that will build stadiums for them. And they often do abandon cities that are recalcitrant. Additionally, a Super Bowl game is often promised to cities that build new stadiums, putting these cities "on the map," as far as the sports world is concerned.

Symbolically, the Super Bowl is similar to all football games in that it deals with taking control of territory, except that the stakes are much higher in the Super Bowl because the team that takes control of the desired territory the most often, and thus scores the most points, wins the championship. Games such as football have often been compared to wars between two armies. But the Super Bowl is pre-eminent because the winner of that game claims to be the world champion football team.

Finally, there is the matter of the Super Bowl as an example of cultural imperialism. The game is broadcast all over the world now, to huge numbers of people who don't really understand the game and who know almost nothing about the players or the teams. The fact that the Super Bowl game is the largest media event of the year is yet another testimony to the power of marketing; the whole world has been colonized to see the commercials created by advertising agencies that sell not only products but, indirectly, the self-proclaimed superiority of free enterprise and American bourgeois capitalism. For the 2001 Super Bowl game, sponsors paid $2.3 million for a 30-second commercial and CBS sold all the time it had for commercials.

# THE SUPER BOWL AS SIGN SYSTEM: A SEMIOTIC PERSPECTIVE

The fact that Roman numerals are used to designate which Super Bowl game is being played is an important semiotic sign. Roman numerals are used to signify importance, status, by connecting an entity to antiquity, to Roman history, and civilization. The use of Roman numerals gives football players in the Super Bowl some kind of gladiatorial aura and, in a way, gives the Super Bowl an air of gravity and importance. It is, after all, only a football game.

In the stadium that hosts the Super Bowl, there is the usual brilliance to the colors—the green grass with white stripes every 10 yards, the uniforms of the players, the costumes of the cheerleaders, the black-and-white striped shirts of the officials and their colorful handkerchiefs, and the clothes worn by the fans. And there is signage everywhere—on each player's uniform, in the gestures used by the officials when there are touchdowns, the advertisements found on the walls of the stadium, and the signs and regalia of the fans.

The Super Bowl game—like all football games—is dramatized by the television director who chooses certain shots to focus on some individual or show reactions by players or coaches to a given play. Some plays are shown from three or four different angles and in some cases they are also diagrammed by one of the commentators. I suggest that the televised version of the Super Bowl, which often employs as many as 30 or so camera crews—many more than ordinary games—is considerably different from the game seen by people at the Super Bowl.

Television directors can show the same shot from several different angles, can zoom in on particular players or coaches and turn the Super Bowl into a psychological thriller. It is this aspect of the televised game, which can approach surrealism, that probably captures the interest of audiences in foreign countries, who know very little about the intricacies of the game itself.

The way directors tend to focus on certain players during the game is an unconscious means of strengthening the hyper-individualism that is so dominant in American culture. The Super Bowl is played by teams, but the television broadcast isolates various heroes and fools (those who make mistakes like fumbling the ball) and uses them to create a sense of drama.

The names of football teams are often symbolic and link the teams to historical events or periods, important totems, wild animals, and so on. With the rise of self-consciousness in certain groups, such as the Native Americans, the names of teams like the Washington Redskins have now become the subject of considerable controversy.

## PSYCHOANALYTIC PERSPECTIVES ON THE SUPER BOWL

The question sports fans are asking now is whether the Super Bowl is—or has somehow become—part of some ritualistic sacrifice of teams from the American Football Conference (AFC) to teams from the National Football Conference (NFC). The NFC seems to be a much stronger conference and its teams have humiliated AFC teams in recent years. The AFC had lost 14 Super Bowls in a row, before they started winning them.

It is also interesting to consider what is at work in the fans of various teams who so strongly identify with their teams. Some fans have a collector's mentality and need for closure: They pride themselves on never missing a home game for various periods of years. These fans often wear clothes with the logos of their team on it and follow the lives of the team's players and coaches with passionate interest. Because Super Bowls are played in various cities, some fans of conference champions don't get to see their teams in the Super Bowl.

This identification serves to make individuals forget that their lives, as the late Senator Fulbright put it so coldly, "are minor events in the ongoing universe." By attaching themselves to their team and to its various heroes, fans give their lives a sense of importance and find an identity. And when their team goes to the Super Bowl, there is a halo effect that is generated.

There is also the matter of the violence that must be considered. This violence is disguised by terms like *tackled* and *sacked* and the rules of the game, which allow for bodily contact. But terms cannot disguise the images of quarterbacks who are shown being sacked, their bodies recoiling in shock with expressions of pain and agony on their faces. Where physical contact ends and violence begins is often difficult to say, but the number of injured players on teams—many of whom can only play because they are given pain killers—is considerable.

Finally, we must consider the boring nature of the game of football. It is a highly routinized and segmented sport, punctuated with huddles and time-outs (especially for television commercials), and characterized by relatively short spurts of action, often lasting no more than a few seconds. The game is, at its roots, about controlling territory and about evasion and breaking free of constraints.

When two teams are evenly matched, the question of who will win the game often becomes interesting and heroic actions by this or that player take on a heightened importance. But in a number of recent Super Bowl games, there has been little drama to speak of; there has merely been the matter of the winning team degrading and intimidating the losing team. This forces the commentators to find topics to discuss that are not immediately related to the game.

## SOCIOLOGICAL ASPECTS OF THE SUPER BOWL

The fact that many of the sites of Super Bowls are tourist and resort areas has already been mentioned; I have suggested that this phenomenon represents the unification of sports (now seen as an entertainment genre) and tourism into a kind of mega-industry. Sports teams and stadiums are now part of the "sell" of cities that wish to attract tourists.

And like tourism, the Super Bowl presents people with an opportunity to display their power and status—first, by having a seat at the Super Bowl, and second, by having a good seat at the Super Bowl. One way people who attend the Super Bowl can measure their status is by calculating how close they were to the 50- yard line . . . or wherever the "best" seats in the stadium are. The high and mighty, of course, are in boxes where they do not have to mingle with the hoi polloi. Those who cannot attend, display their status by throwing "Super" parties.

Super Bowl Sunday, as it is called, represents the power of media to take a commercial entertainment media event and turn it into a quasi-official national holiday. The Super Bowl is the biggest media sports event of the year in America. Unlike the World Series, the Super Bowl is only one game—so it commands the attention of the American public, which is subjected to weeks of hype on the event.

The Super Bowl can also be seen as a functional alternative to a religious holiday. In fact, one can argue that the Super Bowl is essentially a transmogrified religious event, full of Saints (especially when New Orleans is playing) and Sinners (those who fumble or drop easy passes). The same passion, the same feverish excitement that one finds in religious celebrations is found in the Super Bowl—at least at the beginning of the game. And sometimes, when there are successful "Hail Mary" passes, at the end of a game, when a form of "salvation" has been achieved. (I don't wish to push this analogy too far, but I don't think I'm stretching things to notice the passion in fans and the various similarities between football and religion. I have discussed this matter in some detail in Berger, 1998.)

This ritual combat in the Super Bowl reflects American culture's values to a considerable degree. I'm talking about an obsession with winning and being "Number One," an obsession with status and "class," and an obsession with participating in "history."

Thus, there is a concern with identifying with the championship team and obtaining some kind of a "halo" effect, with a game that is the most important one of the year, and with "being there" physically (that gets the most status points) or vicariously, and watching the game.

Some scholars argue that American popular culture and mass media are the only things that help unify an increasingly diverse American society. If that is the case, certainly the Super Bowl ranks high if not "number one" on the list of acculturating and socializing media events in America.

## CONCLUSIONS: A POINT AFTER

The Super Bowl is, as Mike Real (1989) argued, a mythic media event. It is an island of a football game that floats in a huge sea of dialogue and chatter from players, coaches, sports journalists, academics, and fans. And commercials. I have given—using a number of different disciplines—what might be described as a *Rashomonian* interpretation of the Super Bowl, although it might be argued that this kind of analysis should really be saved for RashoMonday Night Football.

# Chapter 5

# *Frasier*
## *A 20th-Century Fool*

This is an analysis of one of the foremost (best written and most brilliantly performed) family of fools in contemporary American popular culture: Frasier, the radio psychiatrist who never gets the girl, and his "family" of fools—his brother, also a psychiatrist, the prissy Niles; his blue-collar (ex-cop) and very sarcastic father, Martin; his father's physical therapist, the slightly wacky Daphne; and Frasier's producer, at the radio station where he works, the beautiful but eternally man-hungry, Roz. There are other fools in the show but they only show up from time to time.

I define a *fool*, incidentally, as a character who is eccentric, who is monomaniacal, who violates the codes of his culture, who is at times self-defeating, who makes bad bargains, who is often victimized, who gets into crazy situations, who is "slapped" endlessly, but also who always recovers. Tragic heroes usually die in Act III, but foolish heroes live on, so they can get slapped down again. And again. And again. But first, a brief disquisition on humor.

## WHY WE LAUGH

Nobody knows why we laugh. For thousands of years, from Aristotle to Freud, from Hobbes to Kant, our greatest minds have speculated about why people laugh. The conclusions these thinkers reached are interesting—but not particularly helpful to writers, except in a rather vague way.

Briefly, these thinkers, and others who have speculated about humor, argued that we laugh because of the following reasons:

1. We feel *superior* to people (those we laugh at).
2. We rejoice in *masked aggression* against assorted victims (a Freudian, psychoanalytic perspective).
3. We find *incongruities* between what we expect and what we get (e.g., punch lines in jokes).
4. We use our *cognitive processes* and find something amusing due to the way that the brain processes information (and tells us when play frames are operating and we shouldn't take insults seriously).

I have a number of books in my library that offer, between them, more than 50 explanations of why we laugh, but they all boil down to some variation on one of these four "why" theories.

## WHAT MAKES US LAUGH

The problem with these why theories is that they don't tell you very much. Anything funny is reduced to one of the four categories just mentioned. But when we laugh at something that happens in a situation comedy like *Frasier,* for example, it is more useful, I argue, to know *what* makes us laugh. And I have, I believe, an answer to that question. Or is it the answer to that question?

A number of years ago, I made a content analysis of everything that I could find that was funny. I looked at books of cartoons, comic books, short stories, novels, plays, joke books . . . asking myself, in each case, "What is it that is generating the humor?" I came up with 45 techniques that I suggest are the essential building blocks of humor.

I analyzed plays by Plautus, written 2,000 years ago, and plays by Shakespeare and Ionesco, who use a good number of the techniques. (I got some of my techniques from them.) I argue that these techniques are used by humorists from all time periods in all genres and all media and probably in all cultures. All humor, from all time periods, in all countries, in all media and all genres, use these 45 techniques because, I suggest, they are the only ones available.

These 45 techniques are often used in combinations, so it isn't unusual to find two or three techniques functioning together to create humor. I am not suggesting that any comedy writers have actually articulated all of these techniques (although some writers have listed some of them) and think about them when they write comedy. All I am suggesting is that they use them.

When I discovered these techniques, I didn't realize that they fell into four categories—language, logic, identity, and a fourth one I described as action, but that also might be described as involving visual humor. Among the most commonly used of these 45 techniques are insult, before and after, repartee, exposure, ridicule, exaggeration, reversal, accident, sarcasm, irony, facetiousness, allusions, mistakes, misunderstandings, and eccentricity. These techniques are listed in Table 5.1.

TABLE 5.1
The 45 Techniques of Humor Arranged According to Category

| Language | Logic | Identity | Action |
|---|---|---|---|
| Allusion | Absurdity | Before/After | Chase |
| Bombast | Accident | Burlesque | Slapstick |
| Definition | Analogy | Caricature | Speed |
| Exaggeration | Catalogue | Eccentricity | |
| Facetiousness | Coincidence | Embarrassment | |
| Insults | Comparison | Exposure | |
| Infantilism | Disappointment | Grotesque | |
| Irony | Ignorance | Imitation | |
| Misunderstanding | Mistakes | Impersonation | |
| Over literalness | Repetition | Mimicry | |
| Puns/wordplay | Reversal | Parody | |
| Repartee | Rigidity | Scale | |
| Ridicule | Theme & var. | Stereotype | |
| Sarcasm | Unmasking | | |
| Satire | | | |

## APPLYING THE TECHNIQUES TO "THE GOOD SON"

Using the techniques to create comedy is just the flip side of applying the techniques to analyze it. Let me offer a few examples of how we can use my techniques to see how writers generate humor in a script. The script I am using is the brilliantly written and very funny *Frasier* pilot script, "The Good Son," written by David Angell, Peter Casey, and David Lee. We must recognize that when we turn on a television set to see a situation comedy, we hope and expect to laugh. So we see everything in terms of a play frame that says—all of these things, like insults and eccentricity, are not to be taken seriously but are only meant to entertain and amuse.

## Eccentricity

At the start of the show we find the following dialogue. Frasier is in the middle of answering a caller:

> FRASIER
> (FIRMLY WITH CONCERN)
> Listen to yourself, Bob. You follow her to work. You eavesdrop on her calls. You open her mail. The minute you started doing these things, the relationship was over.

This dialogue establishes Bob as a real eccentric, a somewhat paranoid individual with an extremely possessive attitude toward his girlfriend. Bob is, in short, a kook, like many of the characters with whom Frasier deals. Comedy often involves fools and eccentrics of one sort or another—people with certain zany monomanias—who interact, with other zanies or with normal people, in amusing ways.

Fools, of course, are not necessarily funny. They have to be put into situations where their foolishness will lead to amusement. Generally speaking, foolishness and eccentricity are combined with other techniques in order to be amusing: insult, exaggeration, reversal, and so on. And in the context of a play frame.

## Definition and Exaggeration

The second caller is Russell, who says he feels like he's in a rut. We hear a voiceover (VO) for Russell.

> RUSSELL (VO)
> Well, I've been feeling, sort of, you know, depressed lately.
>
> FRASIER
> For how long?
>
> RUSSELL (VO)
> Oh, the last 7 or 8 years.

Russell's reply is funny because of his definition of "lately." His "lately" turns out to be 7 or 8 years, which I would suggest combines definition and wild exaggeration.

## Before and After, Unmasking, and Insult

To give listeners a sense of who Frasier is, and what his personality is like, the writers have Frasier talk about himself. It was an extremely clever and economical way to introduce Frasier to listeners. He is replying to someone who has called in and discusses his own life.

> FRASIER
> Let me see if I can cut to the chase by using myself as an example. Six months ago I was living in Boston. My wife had left me, which was very painful, then she came back, which was excruciating.

Here, Frasier reveals something about himself. His wife had left him, which he said was painful. The next line, which is very funny, involves a reversal—she came back, and that, he explained, was excruciating.

I classify this as before (she left him and it was painful) and after (she came back and it was excruciating) and insult. His reaction to her coming back surprises us—we expect they will get together. But Frasier describes it as excruciating; this tops off the original insult.

## Mistakes and Cataloging

I make a distinction between misunderstandings, which are verbal, and mistakes, which are things people do that are wrong, ill-advised, and so on. We find mistakes funny when there is a play frame and we define the mistakes we see as in the realm of humor . . . and not as "serious." Mistakes, by themselves, like all the other techniques, are not necessarily funny. Generally, the technique has to be supported by others techniques, too, such as exaggeration and cataloging.

At the end of the scene, Frasier asks Roz how he did:

> ROZ
> Did I ever show you what this button does?
>
> FRASIER
> I'm not a piece of Lalique. I can handle criticism. How was I today?

> ROZ
>
> Let's see. You dropped two commercials, you left a total of 28 seconds of dead air, you scrambled the station's call letters, you spilled yogurt on the control board, and you kept referring to Jerry with the identity crisis as "Jeff."

This discussion of techniques doesn't deal with an important element of comedy—the way actors and actresses speak their lines, use facial expressions and body language, and that kind of thing. But without good lines, which come from creating interesting and somewhat zany characters, locked into relationships that enable writers to generate humor, even the best performers find it difficult to be funny. My system does not concern itself with narrative structure, either. In *Frasier* there are often surprising resolutions or clever lines at the end of the shows, that end them with a bit of a punch. The reference to Lalique offers an insight into Frasier, also—he has a sense of refinement that is rather precious.

## Insults and Repartee

Consider the characters in the show. Frasier and his brother Niles, also somewhat of an eccentric, have a relationship based on love and insults. Here's a confrontation between Frasier and Niles:

> NILES
>
> You know what I think about pop psychiatry.
>
> FRASIER
>
> Yes, yes, I know what you think about everything. When was the last time you had an unexpressed thought?

This friendly banter shows the relationship between the brothers and also gives some insights into Niles' personality. Niles, we can infer, thinks pop psychiatry is a waste of time. This is an indirect insult and put down. Frasier answers that he knows what Niles thinks about everything, an example of repartee.

Frasier is a somewhat pompous fool and thus ripe for continually being deflated. Additionally, Frasier has a relationship with his father, Martin, that is more or less like Frasier's relationship with Niles, except that Martin is much more sarcastic and direct. Martin is a retired cop, who has been shot and generally must use a cane or crutch to get around. His tastes are very blue collar. He doesn't have the same sensibilities as his more sophisticated sons. This is an important complication because Martin lives with Frasier.

**Revelation of Character and Reversal**

Niles, also a psychiatrist, is also a bit odd. Niles is married to Maris, a woman we never see. We only hear about her. And he develops a crush on Daphne, the woman hired to take care of Martin. We are introduced to Niles with the following lines

> NILES (VO)
> So I said to the gardener, "Yoshi, I do not need a Zen garden in my backyard. . . . If I want to rake gravel every 10 minutes to maintain my inner harmony, I'll move to Yokohama." . . . Well, this offends him so he starts pulling up Maris' prized camellias by the handful. I couldn't stand that, so I marched right into the morning room and locked the door until he cooled down.

First of all, we discover that Niles and his wife have a Japanese gardener, Yoshi, who wants to make their back garden into something approximating a Zen temple. They are revealed, then, as somewhat trendy, well-to-do types. Niles is a weakling and perhaps a bit prissy. Instead of doing something to stop Yoshi, Niles says, rather proudly it seems, "I marched right into the morning room and locked the door until he cooled down," suggesting that Niles avoids confrontations and is a coward. He is, in addition, a bit of a prig, as well. The line about Yoshi "cooling down" is another example of how the writers play with the viewers and defeat their expectations by reversing things. We would normally expect that Niles would be talking about himself cooling down.

By casting Frasier as a radio psychiatrist, the writers are able to bring on all kinds of weird characters, too—as voiceovers. Thus, there are almost infinite possibilities for introducing zanies onto the show. Even Martin's dog, Eddie, who stares at Frasier all the time, is odd. So what we have is a collection of fools—of eccentric and odd characters, with various monomaniacal fixations and quirks, who can play off one another in endless permutations and combinations . . . and who play off the relatively normal characters in the show. The women are a bit daffy, too—Roz (who has this fixation about finding a man) and Daphne (who is a bit of a psychic). Also, we must remember Niles' wife Maris, who is not in the show, but who is often talked about, ridiculed, and insulted.

## Insults and Analogy

In the following lines we see how the technique of insult is used. Frasier and Niles are talking about where to put their father and Maris' name comes up.

> NILES
> Dad doesn't get along with Maris.
>
> FRASIER
> Who does?
>
> NILES
> I thought you liked my Maris.
>
> FRASIER
> I do. I like her from a distance. You know, the way you like the sun. Maris is like the sun . . . except without the warmth.

Here, Frasier is using insult and analogy to create the humor. Nobody likes Maris. She's cold—or as Frasier puts it, "like the sun . . . except without the warmth." So she is set up as a person who will be the butt of many digs and insults.

A great deal of humor, I should point out, involves techniques that don't necessarily lead to loud outbursts of laughter but, instead, smiles and amusement. Once characters establish themselves, writers can refine and develop their personalities. When Jack Benny discovered there was mileage in being cheap, his writers were able to use that eccentric persona in all kinds of different ways and tie exaggeration and various other techniques to it. Kelsey Grammer, who plays Frasier, is a big fan of Jack Benny, one of the greatest fool figures American popular culture has produced.

## The Figure in the Carpet

Comedy writers don't necessarily bring any of these techniques to consciousness, but that doesn't mean they don't use them. I think that comedy writers learn, through experience, what works in given situations. The difference between great comedy writers and mediocre ones involves the sophistication and creativity that they bring to their writing which means, I argue, the degree to which they can use the various comedy techniques in clever and interesting ways.

Comedy is the hardest kind of writing. It is very difficult to make people laugh—even if they want to laugh. So it isn't surprising that most sitcoms aren't successful. In a sense, my techniques need the right kind of dramatic personalities to work very well. But if you look at some of the best scripts for sitcoms and if you look at some of the greatest dramatic comedies, you'll see that the all of the writers used a number of the techniques and used them brilliantly. I'm thinking of plays such as William Shakespeare's *Twelfth Night* or Ben Jonson's *Volpone* or Eugene Ionesco's *Bald Soprano* or Tom Stoppard's *Travesties*.

You don't have to be aware that there's such a thing as schizophrenia to be crazy. And if you are a comedy writer, you don't have to be aware of my techniques to be funny, but you can't be funny without using the techniques in various combinations and permutations that generate humor. And there are no other techniques that I have been able to find. (In some cases, such as victim humor, we have insult humor that is reversed. Some of the techniques can be reversed.) The writers for *Frasier* do know how to use these techniques, and they often use them brilliantly, even if they are not consciously thinking about them, which explains why the show has been so successful. It's how you use the techniques that makes the difference. In the case of *Frasier,* the creators of the show had a recognized character—from *Cheers*. But they were able to invent a family of fools equally as zany and eccentric, in their way, as Frasier. And that family has won endless number of awards and kept millions of Americans laughing in one of the most literate and beautifully realized of recent American situation comedies.

The creators of *Frasier* were very wise and very lucky in their choice of fools.

# Chapter 6

# *Bloopers*
## *What They Are and What They Mean*

Out of the mouths of babes come wonders. Bloopers are traditionally understood as statements, not meant to be humorous, that are, for one reason or another, very amusing. That is because the people making the bloopers (usually children and young students but also college students and adults) make spelling errors, write faulty grammatical constructions, speak malapropisms, and offer inane definitions—among other things—that massacre, in an accidentally humorous manner, our common knowledge and history.

### KINDS OF BLOOPERS

Bloopers are a form of accidental or found humor, based on mistakes people make in using language and expressing their thoughts and ideas:

> **Mistakes in spelling:** *The Roman Spear of Influence*
> **Mistakes in word usage:** *Magellan was the first man to circumcise the globe.*
> **Mistakes in grammatical constructions:** *Tuesday at 4 p.m. there will be an ice cream social. All ladies giving milk will please come early.*

> **Mistakes in comparisons and analogies:** *Annuals are flowers used for weddings; perennials are flowers used for funerals.*
> **Mistakes in knowledge:** *Monkeys and man both belong to the order of pirates.*
> **Mistakes in definitions:** *Germinate means to become a nationalized German.*

and various other kinds of mistakes and combinations of mistakes. In a number of cases, bloopers come from attempts children make to figure out what terms mean—as in the germinate definition.

So one important fact about bloopers, as I previously pointed out, is that they are funny even though they weren't meant to be funny. We get bloopers from many different sources: mistakes students make in the tests they take at school, in the answers they give to questions in classroom discussions, from statements people make during conversations, and from notices that people write in publications.

## WHY WE LAUGH AT BLOOPERS

Why do we laugh at bloopers? It might be because we feel a sense of superiority (if only for a moment) over those who make them, revealing their innocence or naiveté. We find bloopers funny because we know the difference between what was written or said and what was meant, or between what was written or said and what the truth of the matter is.

In other cases, we recognize that children makes all kinds of innocent mistakes that are understandable, such as assuming God's name is Harold!

> *Our father, who art in heaven, Harold be thy name.*

There is a kind of discrepant awareness at work. Readers of bloopers are aware of correct spellings, correct information, and so on—otherwise they wouldn't recognize that the blooper is a mistake of one kind or another and wouldn't find bloopers amusing. Let me suggest, then, that there are two opposing groups involved in the blooper making–laughing at blooper process.

| **Blooper Maker** | **Blooper Audience** |
|---|---|
| Makes mistakes | Knows correct answers |
| Ignorance | Knowledge |

| | |
|---|---|
| Naiveté, innocence | Sophistication |
| Error | Truth |
| Creativity | Custom and consensus |
| Childhood, youth | Adulthood |

Most of the bloopers made by children involve a lack of information, innocence, and naiveté, whereas those made by adults are based on faulty grammatical constructions, although we also find occasional spelling mistakes and typos.

The list just presented suggests that another reason we laugh at bloopers is because of the incongruity between what we expect (the real definition of a word) and what we get (the blooper definition), between truth (what we expect) and error (what we get). Blooper makers are, it could be said, making fools of themselves without recognizing that they are doing so.

Sometimes, curiously enough, the bloopers, even though they are based on humorous mistakes, reveal interesting truths. Thus, there is a wonderful realism in the blooper that tells us that:

*Christian Science is a religion where they cure you by saying good things about you, even if there aren't any.*

It's the last phrase in this definition that is crucial. Yes, there actually are people about whom nothing good can be said—such as (as any college professor could tell you) deans and college presidents . . . or as deans and college presidents could tell you, professors.

## BLOOPERS AS A FORM OF LIBERATION

There may also be an element in participating in the accidental and unconscious aggression, created by blooper makers and found in their bloopers, against civilization and its standards and notions of correctness. Bloopers offer a momentary liberation for us that not only amuses us but makes us more sanguine about the human condition and our possibilities. Bloopers reinforce our notion of human freedom and contingency. It can be argued that our ability to make bloopers frees us from being constrained in the "iron cage of reason" and adds a measure of color and humanity to our lives.

It is possible in some cases that certain bloopers are actually "put-ons" in which students purposely create bloopers (or use ones they have heard or read) as a kind of joke on their teachers. Or teachers "invent" bloopers. But let us assume that most bloopers are the real thing—and enjoy them as expressions of the human spirit and our invincible ignorance.

## A PERSONAL NOTE FROM A LOVER OF BLOOPERS

I started teaching at the university level in 1961, when I went to graduate school at the University of Minnesota to get my doctorate in American studies. Because my master's degree was in journalism from the University of Iowa (although I also had studied at the Writers Workshop there), the head of Freshman English decided I shouldn't be allowed to teach literature sections and so I was relegated to Composition X—that is what is commonly known as "bonehead English."

It was while teaching this course that I had one of my most wonderful experiences with the blooperish mind of some college students. At the end of the semester, I asked my students to write an evaluation of the course and one student recounted a recent experience he had that he thought I would find interesting. I should point out that I used to ride a bicycle and had bought an old ammunition bag, in a surplus store, in which I carried my books.

He wrote:

> I was walking in the Quad last week with my friend Joe and we saw you riding by on your bike with your ammunition bag. My friend Joe pointed to you, then turned to me and said, "Look at that red-headed idiot riding by." I turned to him, and said proudly, "That red-headed idiot happens to be my Composition X teacher!"

It was the "and said proudly" that warmed my heart. This student went on, I would hazard a guess, to make some wonderful bloopers. He had what we can all recognize, I think, as a really first-class blooper-making mind.

I have taught writing for many years, but I have never had a student give me quite as lovely a compliment. And I suspect that his statement, in a rather remarkable way, prepared me for the rigors I would face in the next 35 years of academic life.

## ENJOY, ENJOY!

I hope you enjoy the bloopers I offer here (taken from the Internet and various other sources) and find them amusing, entertaining, and a wonderful reflection of the comedy of errors that we find in everyday life. You can see in these bloopers, evidence of minds that are struggling—generally unsuccessfully—to make sense of things. You can see in them evidence of minds trying to figure out answers, generally incorrectly, to questions. You can see minds improvising definitions that are far-fetched and ridiculous but often, in a strange way, quite wonderful.

Bloopers are superb testimonials to the human genius for screwing up in different ways. The 2000 presidential election is a remarkable example of the human capacity to make a mess of things. A short while after I was drafted into the U.S. Army (yes, I am a trained killer), I learned that there are three ways to do things:

> *the right way*
> *the wrong way, and*
> *the Army way.*

Now, in an age of hucksterism, multiculturalism, and media, we can add three other ways:

> *the Amway,*
> *the Zimbabwe, and for the media wise,*
> *the segue.*

For those who read the Old Testament, we can add yet another:

> *the Yahweh.*

## THE ETHICAL PROBLEM

While I was collecting my bloopers (and I had help from a number of people sending e-mail messages and from the Internet), some people raised the question of whether printing bloopers was ethical. Offering bloopers to readers, it was suggested, was demeaning and a means of exploiting students. Others disagreed and a lively debate took place as e-mail messages flew back and forth.

Because no students are mentioned by name, and because we all recognize that people at all ages make mistakes (in fact, the comedy of error is one of the building blocks of humor, as Shakespeare's plays demonstrate), collecting amusing bloopers should be looked on as an attempt to bring a bit more humor and humanity into our lives—a most ethical consideration, if you ask me. If you can't laugh at others, you can't laugh at yourself. And being able to laugh at oneself is, psychologists tell us, a very important matter.

Because bloopers tend to be made in academic settings, they can be classified according to the subjects they deal with. Accordingly, I offer a brief survey of some of the more common topics of bloopers—history, science, religion, and so on—and some good examples of bloopers dealing with these subjects. In some cases, a blooper can legitimately be placed in more than one category. Where a blooper belongs isn't terribly important; what is important is that the blooper be amusing.

In Jorge Luis Borges' (1968) *Other Inquisitions: 1937-1952*, he described a Chinese encyclopedia, the *Celestial Emporium of Benevolent Knowledge*,

> in which it is written that animals are divided into (a) those that belong to the emperor, (b) embalmed ones, (c) those that are trained, (d) suckling pigs, (e) mermaids, (f) fabulous ones, (g) stray dogs, (h) those that are included in this classification, (i) those that tremble as if they were mad, (j) innumerable ones, (k) those drawn with a very fine camel's hair brush, (l) others, (m) those that have just broken a flower vase, (n) those that resemble flies from a distance. (p. 103)

In dealing with the bloopers I use in this chapter, also a collection of benevolent knowledge, I have a less complicated classification system. I have taken the bloopers and classified them into nine categories: history, religion, science, literature and art, love, philosophy, health, politics, and definitions.

## BLOOPERS ABOUT HISTORY

These are, I suggest, the basic subjects the bloopers deal with. My first category, history, deals with important figures in the past and events of significance. We learn, for example, that:

*Magellan was the first man to circumcise the globe,*

a remarkable achievement, no doubt, although it is hard to determine how he did it and what it means. Mohels, who perform Jewish ritual circumcisions, must be awestricken by the enormity of Magellan's accomplishment.

We also learn that:

*The Revolution against the British was led by Manhattan Dandy,*

a not-too-close approximation of Mahatma Gandhi, although, by chance, correct as far as the "dandy" part is concerned (in his early years, that is). Part of the amusement from bloopers comes from the heroic but highly erratic attempts children (and others) make to answer questions. In other bloopers, something else generates the humor.

Consider, for example, the following:

*Queen Elizabeth was known as the "Virgin Queen." As a Queen she was a great success.*

What this blooper implies, due to its wording, is that as a virgin, Queen Elizabeth was not a great success . . . a most amusing idea. Blooper makers are all revisionist historians who give us something to laugh about, and occasionally, something to think about.

## BLOOPERS ABOUT RELIGION

The bloopers in this section consist of some bloopers evidently made by children, who are trying, as best they can, to answer questions that have been asked of them. In some cases, they rely on their wits to figure out answers. Thus we find:

*The first man to go on the Crusades was Robinson Crusoe.*

We can understand how this blooper was made. The child (or whoever it was) who made this blooper saw a connection between the word "Crusade" and the name "Crusoe," and so, putting two and two together, thought Robinson Crusoe was the first man to go on the Crusades.

In other cases, children make mistakes in using language that are most amusing. We learn, for example, about how Christianity impacted on marriage:

*In Christianity a man can have only one wife. That is known as Monotony.*

Whether this mistake, ironically, expresses an insight or even a truth about monogamous marriage is something I leave for those who are married to decide.

The second kind of blooper comes from messages on Church bulletin boards or in materials sent to congregants—errors made by adults in the wording or construction of sentences. We find, for example:

*Thursdays at 5 p.m. there will be a meeting of the Little Mothers Club. All wishing to become Little Mothers should see the minister in his study.*

This message amuses us because, by mistake, it suggests sexual relations between the minister and his congregants who wish to become "Little Mothers." Clergymen, in all religions, being human, sometimes are tempted into sexual dalliances with their congregants and do, at times, create "little mothers," but this blooper does not mean to suggest this. It is the ambiguity of the language in this blooper, which allows us to read things into the message, that creates the humor.

The blooper

*Thursday Night Potluck Supper. Prayer and Medication to follow.*

is a typographical error that strikes us as an unwitting revelation about the quality of Church potluck suppers.

One of the religious bloopers in this chapter,

*The prevailing religion in England is Hypocrisy*

is, like so many bloopers, a mistake that reveals an important truth—perhaps not only about religion in England but other places as well.

## BLOOPERS ABOUT SCIENCE

When blooper makers turn their attention to science, we get some truly remarkable statements. These bloopers deal with botany, geology, mathematics, chemistry, and other related areas. Once again, these bloopers reveal the way young minds attempt to make sense of things and use what knowledge they possess to answer questions.

In one case, when asked about quinine, the blooper maker knew that it comes from the bark of trees.

*Quinine comes from the bark of trees. Canine comes from the bark of a dog.*

The word endings "ine" and the term "bark" led the blooper maker to a logical conclusion. If quinine comes from the bark of trees, canine, logically, should or is it could (?) come from the bark of dogs, except, of course, that we have two different kinds of "barks" here.

The remarkable insight into the relations between the sexes expressed in the following blooper should give us all something to think about:

> *When birds quarrel, it is usually the female bird, as with humans, that comes out the winner.*

How did our blooper maker gain this remarkable piece of wisdom? It is the tangential remark, "as with humans," that gives this blooper its cultural and social resonance. As is often the case, the matter is stated in absolutes—not "as is often the case with humans" but in a strong manner, "as with humans." We are, in some ways, like birds and philosophers have, at one time or another, described humans as "featherless bipeds." Maybe that's the connection?

One of my favorite science bloopers is:

> *Sturgeon are cartilaginous gonads with long nostrums.*

It has a wonderful technical ring to it and is stated in an authoritative tone, but like much that has the same technological aura, it is complete nonsense. We might suspect this, because as another science blooper teaches us:

> *Sound is a vapid series of osculations.*

Too often, alas, that is the case.

## BLOOPERS ON LITERATURE AND ART

When we come to literature (and an occasional excursion into art), our blooper makers offer us many interesting notions and remarkable insights. As one blooper maker explains:

> *Tennyson betrayed women very successfully.*

This blooper is based on mistaking "betrayed" for "portrayed," but it may also be that our blooper maker was correct. It certainly is a point that is worth investigating by literary scholars, and literary biographers, in particular.

The blooper about Wordsworth is also worth considering with more care:

> *Wordsworth's most famous poem is "Imitations of Immorality in Youth."*

There is no question that youth is often immoral, although Wordsworth's poem is not quite what our blooper maker would have us think it is. In order to see the humor in this blooper, one must be familiar with Wordsworth and know what the title of his poem actually was. Our blooper maker got a couple of the words wrong, and that makes all the difference in the world.

This calls our attention to the matter of knowledge and ignorance. Bloopers presuppose a certain amount of knowledge—so we can see how the blooper maker has erred. If you do not know the correct title of Wordsworth's poem, you don't see how funny the blooper is. Bloopers are often incongruous imitations, unwitting parodies, unrecognized mistakes, and misinterpretations, and we have to recognize what is being done in a blooper to see the humor.

In the blooper that follows,

*"La Belle Dame Sans Merci" means "the beautiful lady who never said 'Thank you,'"*

we have someone with a rudimentary knowledge of French translating the title of a poem. "La Belle Dame" means "beautiful lady." "Sans Merci" doesn't mean "who never said Thank you" but means "without mercy." "Sans" means "without," not "who never said." "Merci" has to be understood in the context of the poem, not the term "Merci," which can mean "thank you." In this blooper, we find the truth of the statement that "a little bit of knowledge can get you into a lot of trouble."

## BLOOPERS ON PHILOSOPHY AND PHILOSOPHICAL CONCERNS

These bloopers were made by college students who were answering questions posed to them by their professors. Some of the answers may give those of us with a philosophical bent, much to think about.

Many of the bloopers that follow have an Ionesco-esque, "theater of the absurd," quality. In *The Bald Soprano,* Ionesco had one of his characters speculate about why newspapers give the ages of people when they die but don't give the ages of people when they are born. In like manner, we find one of young philosophers informing us:

*Before we are born, our consciences probably do not exist.*

Notice how clever this philosopher is in qualifying the assertion. He or she does not write "our consciences do not exist" but "our consciences probably do not exist." This is in the best philosophical tradition, which teaches us, among other things, to question all knowledge.

Another philosopher informs us:

*We don't worry about the times before we were born because our lives then had no importance.*

Here the tone is much more assertive, and with good reason, too. The writer is absolutely correct. Before we were born . . . our lives had no importance. That is an indisputable fact, unless, of course, you believe in reincarnation and believe people have many lives, in which case our lives, before we were born, had great importance.
One of our student philosophers of education offers us an ambivalent view of things:

*As to the core curriculum, there are pros and cons for it and pros and cons against it.*

This student philosopher could have benefitted, let me suggest, from a core curriculum that involved critical thinking and learning the meaning of words.

## BLOOPERS ON HEALTH AND WELL-BEING

When we come to the subject of health and well-being, our blooper makers are in rare form. There is an old joke revealing our anxiety about doctors, which goes "the operation was a success, but the patient died." Another bit of wisdom tells us that "doctors bury their mistakes." Many of our blooper makers probably will have great careers ahead of them in medicine. Like the doctors in these jokes, these blooper makers inadvertently kill off many of those they are trying to help.
Thus, we learn:

*For asphyxiation, apply artificial respiration until the patient is dead.*

And we gain the following practical advice about nosebleeds:

*For a nosebleed, put the nose much lower than the body until the heart stops.*

Our young proto-physicians are not much kinder to animals:

> *For a dog bite, put the dog away for several days. If it has not recovered, kill it.*

The advice does not deal with humans who have been bitten, notice, but with dogs. For young children, dogs probably are much higher in the Great Chain of Being than humans. And with good reason, too.

Dealing with women calls for the greatest delicacy. One blooper maker faced the problem of what to do with people who fainted. He or she had no problem with men—rub their chests. But what was to be done with women? It would be indelicate, at the very least, to rub their chests. The answer we get is most instructive:

> *If a man faints, rub his chest. If a lady faints, rub her arm above her hand . . . or put her head between the legs of the nearest medical doctor.*

This practice is no longer encouraged, so I've been told, although some doctors might find it quite stimulating . . . and perhaps some "old-fashioned" doctors still encourage it.

## BLOOPERS ABOUT POLITICS

I have separated politics from history, however, there are some who claim that "history is past politics and politics is present history." Our blooper makers tell us that the Constitution gives us some incredible rights. As they write:

> *One right Americans enjoy under the Constitution is the right to keep bare arms.*

This, I might add, is the same justification nudists in America use, although they push the matter well beyond bare arms.

One blooper maker offers a blooper that also could have been put in the chapter on love and romance. In some cases it was difficult to decide into which classification a blooper fell, and thus, occasionally, you may feel my placement of bloopers is somewhat arbitrary. Thus, we learn:

> *The Constitution was adopted to secure domestic hostility in the United States of America.*

There is no question in my mind that a great deal of domestic hostility exists in the United States, but I'm not sure it is because we

have a Constitution. It is, more likely, a matter of our constitutions (those of men and women, parents and children, cats and dogs, etc.).
One blooper deals with state politics:

*Al Capone is the senator from New York.*

The blooper maker who wrote:

*The seats of all Senators are to be vaccinated every 6 years*

had a very good idea, whose time, I believe, will come. The AMA is, so I understand, working on it, even as I write.

## BLOOPERS THAT ARE DEFINITIONS

Definitions are one of the most common forms of bloopers—perhaps because young children are often asked to define words in school. There is no absolute definition of a word; definitions are all based on conventions. So it is possible that some day, the definitions we see in this chapter, will be found in dictionaries. But I wouldn't hold my breath waiting for this to happen.
We learn that some definers mix things together, as in the definition of vacuum that follows:

*Vacuum: a large, empty space where the Pope lives.*

In other cases, blooper makers get a bit mixed up:

*A polygon is a man who has married many women.*

Does that mean, may I ask parenthetically, that a square is a person who has only married one woman?
Some blooper makers use what information they possess, sometimes garbled, to make sense of words:

*A goblet is a male turkey. A giblet is a female turkey.*

What has happened is that the blooper maker mistook the sound turkeys are said to make in America, "Gobble, gobble . . ." with goblets. Then, knowing that there are such things as giblets, our blooper maker put things together.
I like the way the boy scout creed has been mangled in:

*A boyscout is a fiend to all and a bother to all other scouts.*

There are, of course, some boy scouts who are fiends and some scout leaders who are a bother to all (or many) other scouts, but leaving out the letter "r" in this definition leads to hilarious results.

The blooper that concludes this section is, in its own way, a remarkable insight:

*All brutes are imperfect animals. Man alone is a perfect beast.*

It might have been wise to qualify this assertion a bit and say "many men are perfect beasts while the others are imperfect beasts." But this qualified statement lacks the blunt force of the blooper it is based on, which seems to sum everything up very nicely.

## Chapter 7

# *Decoding Everyday Life*

In this chapter, I analyze and "decode" a number of aspects of everyday life, showing the degree to which they are based on codes and structures that most of us are unaware of and never think about. I offer these analyses to suggest that there are interesting aspects of our everyday lives that often escape our attention. We should keep in mind what historian J. Huizinga (1924) pointed out in his book, *Waning of the Middle Ages*:

> The Middle Ages never forgot that all things would be absurd if their meaning were exhausted in their function and their place in the phenomenal world, if their essence did not reach into a world beyond this. This idea of a deeper significance in ordinary things is familiar to us as well, independently of religious convictions: as an indefinite feeling which may be called up at any moment, by the sound of raindrops on the leaves or by the lamplight on a table.

With Huizinga's insight informing my analysis, let me consider my first subject—cigarette smoking.

### CIGARETTE SMOKING

For the first object of my analysis, I take a very common activity, or, as is seen here, series of what might be called micro-activities—the smoking of a cigarette. It is something hundreds of millions of people do every day for a wide variety of reasons, yet, like so much in everyday life, with very little thought to what they are doing and how they are doing it. From our point of view, smoking is a ritualized activity composed of a number of smaller acts that are the fundamental units of the ritual. These acts are learned by watching others.

We start by breaking the activity up into its fundamental acts. What I am doing is listing each act in a typical process known as "having a smoke" or "smoking." The acts are listed in order of occurrence:

1. taking a pack of cigarettes
2. opening it up
3. selecting a cigarette
4. putting a cigarette in the mouth
5. returning the pack to pocket or purse
6. taking a lighter or packet of matches
7. lighting the cigarette—puffing to start the tobacco burning
8. returning the lighter to pocket or purse
9. puffing on cigarette
10. taking the cigarette out of one's mouth to exhale, flick ashes, etc.
11. grinding out the butt in an ashtray or flicking the butt away when done.

There are nearly a dozen acts involved in smoking a cigarette. These acts can be subsumed under four different categories: selecting, lighting, smoking, and disposing. The actual smoking of a cigarette occurs at the end of a relatively long sequence of acts that lead to the consumption of the cigarette, and it is all these little acts that give the smoking of a cigarette a number of gratifications beyond that of puffing away on burning tobacco.

Along with the acts one must go through to smoke there are various social codes connected with smoking. For example, a person smoking in company will often ask people if they would like to have one of the cigarettes. Lately, now that many smokers have been made conscious of the fact that smoking irritates people and secondhand smoke causes cancer, smokers will ask if it is permissible to smoke. The rules of etiquette also suggest that men should light cigarettes for women. In America, now, smoking is not permitted in public buildings and the workplace so smokers are forced to smoke outdoors or in special rooms designated for smoking.

The functions of smoking are numerous; it is an activity that gives people something to do with their hands to relieve boredom or anxiety, it helps confer identity, or, rather, aids in giving a person an image. The brand of cigarette people smoke is a "message" about themselves—a kind of statement they make to the world about how they see themselves. Different brands of cigarettes use advertising to cultivate different images, so a person can choose from ready-made images and identities by smoking a particular brand of cigarette. Marlboro, once a ladies cigarette, has become identified (thanks to advertising) with cowboys, ruggedness, nature, and that kind of thing, whereas Virginia Slims projects an image of sophisticated adult femininity. Cigarettes may also help assuage oral needs in people and be a kind of reverse (in that they are cancer creating) substitute for the mother's breast.

There may also be a sense of the demonic and magical, as people transform themselves into smoke-snorting monsters and dragons. An examination of the four categories under which the 11 acts involved in smoking can be grouped reveals that smoking also is connected to power urges, and smoking may be a kind of power-redeeming substitute for people who, in fact, have little power. (This thesis would suggest that working-class people would be more addicted to smoking than professional people, which happens to be the case.)

The fact that all of these indications are petty and trivial is beside the point. What is revealed is that the various kinds of acts involved in smoking involve different kinds of power: decision making, summoning fire (a kind of magic), destroying or wasting conspicuously, and relegating something to the ash heap.

If we adopt the dramatic metaphor and see our actions as a kind of "theater," in which we are the heroes and heroines (or, at least the leading men and women), smoking can be likened to a performance one puts on, involving a number of props—matches or lighters, cigarettes, ashtrays, and so on. This performance involves a variety of physical actions:

1. opening something
2. picking out something with one's thumb and fingers
3. placing an object to one's lips
4. scratching (matches) or pressing (lighter)
5. sucking on something
6. blowing out smoke
7. flicking ashes away
8. pressing or grinding a butt into an ashtray

and all of these actions can be done in different ways, with different "styles." In addition, there is the matter of where the cigarette is placed in the mouth (left side, center, right side), the angle at which it "dangles," how puffs are taken and the smoke exhaled, the length of the cigarette, its color, whether it has a filter tip or not, and how the cigarette is held.

What is interesting is that smokers usually develop a routine and style of smoking and keep it for as long as they smoke, so that once the act is "gotten together" or the performance is created, the actors keeps on playing the role until they die or stop smoking. Because smoking involves so many different acts and confers, in subtle ways, so many psychic gratifications on the smoker-performer, it is hard to stop smoking. The addiction is, my analysis suggests, more than physical; it is also psychological—nobody likes to leave show biz! This analysis would indicate that in order to stop smoking, we must find substitute rituals, which allow people to "perform" and which take care of power needs they have. That is why chewing gum is so unsatisfactory. It is much too elemental and has connotations of childishness.

Rituals like smoking, then, are chains of actions or sequences of actions that can be examined in terms of their structure as well as their functions. They are coded behavior, and understanding the code helps us to understand the meaning of the ritual. The same kind of structural analysis can be applied to myths, folktales, and various popular art forms—all of which have a variety of elements in combination. In fact, there are an immense number of activities that are part of what is commonly called "everyday life" that are accessible to this technique.

## TRAFFIC SIGNALS

In his book, *Claude Lévi-Strauss*, Edmund Leach (1970) used traffic signals as a way of explicating structural analysis, so this discussion is based on ideas that are not my own. (Leach said that Lévi-Strauss has not used the example of traffic signals but if he did, he would have explained them as Leach does.) Traffic signals are useful because they are part of everyday experience and because they can be explained in a relatively simple manner. Structuralism involves looking at entities in terms of their components and how they are organized.

The basic problem traffic lights solve is that of stopping and starting cars; those are the two polarities. In between, mediating between stopping and starting cars, we have the matter of slowing them down so they can stop. To do this job we have taken the colors red, green, and yellow for stopping, starting, and slowing cars. It is our selection of the color red that has led to our choice of the other colors, and, as Leach pointed out, most of us have been taught to feel that green is the opposite of red the way white is the opposite of black.

The system is not symmetrical in that there is not a separate signal to tell drivers when the red light is going to end and to "mediate" between stopping and starting. This is because it is vital that all cars going in a given direction stop at the same time, but it isn't vital that they start at the same time.

Leach noted that red signifies danger in a variety of different situations—stop signs on roads, hot water, live electricity, and so on. This is because, he suggested, red has a "natural association" with blood, not only in our culture but also in many other cultures. Once we have decided that red is to mean stop, we then find its opposite and use that to mean go. Actually, if you look at a chart of the primary colors—the colors from which all other colors can be made—you find that green is the "opposite" of red. The three primary colors are red, blue, and yellow; they cannot be made from other colors. If we make a color triangle we see that green comes out opposite red.

## Oppositions in Colors

Thus, from the point of view of the color charts, green is the opposite of red. The problem we face now is how to explain the choice of yellow, as the color to mean slow, to mediate between red and green. If you look at the color chart, you can see that orange would not be a good color, in that it is too close to red. Orange is made from red and yellow. The question that arises now is why weren't the three primary colors chosen: red (for stop), blue (for go), and yellow (for slow)? One reason is that blue is closer to red than green; it is not its opposite.

## Traffic-Signal Color Triangle (After Leach)

What we find is that in terms of *luminosity,* yellow is high and green is low; and in terms of *wave lengths*, green is short and red is long. There are, then, oppositions between yellow and green and green and red, when you examine these colors in terms of their luminosity or their wave lengths.

This system of relationships—with oppositions and a mediating element—is, structuralists argue, the key to understanding all kinds of phenomena. As Leach said:

This particular example has not, so far as I am aware, ever been used by Lévi-Strauss, but the structuralist thesis is that triangles of this kind, implying comparable transformations of models of nature as apprehended by human brains, have very general application, though in the general case the possibilities are more complicated. (p. 19)

In the case of traffic signals, Leach mentioned there are a number of possibilities that might have been used:

| **STOP** | **CAUTION** | **GO** |
|---|---|---|
| *red* | *yellow* | *green* |

**Actual sequence**

------------------------------------

| red | green | yellow |
|---|---|---|
| yellow | red | green |
| yellow | green | red |
| green | yellow | red |
| green | red | yellow |

**Other Possible Sequences**

------------------------------------

Leach said that because the colors and their associations are "given" in this case, we don't have to pay any attention to the other possibilities; but in general cases, we do. The key to the game is to discern "how relations which exist in nature (and are apprehended as such by human brains) are used to generate cultural products which incorporate these same relations" (p. 20). From this perspective, all kinds of different aspects of life—our clothes, the food we eat, our myths and folktales (both natural and mass-mediated)—are susceptible to structural analysis, although the relationships are not always as clear as in the case of traffic signals.

The matter is further complicated by the fact that people are often unaware of the significance of what they do; they often do not realize that they are sending messages or that the messages they are sending are different from what they think they are sending.

Words convey meanings; but they don't convey very much information until we have several words and, thereby, meanings related to one another. The same applies to traffic signals and all kinds of other signals, signs, and other forms of communicating we do, whether we recognize this or not.

## PATHWAYS AND OPPOSITIONS IN THE SUPERMARKET

The supermarket is an all-pervasive institution in American culture, and the home of many rituals. From our perspective, here, shopping is not just a random activity but a highly structured one in which the consumer is led, unsuspecting, along pre-selected pathways. The supermarket is a *labyrinth* through which we wander, and our movement in this maze is much more preordained or programmed than we might imagine. I also believe that supermarkets are kinds of "media" that broadcast, so to speak, foods and related items. They use other media—the newspapers and television—to advertise, but they are themselves media in that they carry something and spread it to a public. We can look at supermarkets in terms of their logical structure and we find the following polarities:

| **Periphery** | **Center** |
|---|---|
| Basic foods | Household products |
| High volume foods | Low volume foods |
| Perishables | Staples |
| Short life | Long Life |
| Red meat, dairy | Canned vegetables, pet food |

The supermarket is a study in oppositions of different kinds—they sell food, but also a large number of household items. (The typical supermarket now often stocks more than 20,000 items from all over and has a kind of universality that makes a supermarket a fascinating subject of study.)

The basic opposition is between money and merchandise for it is money that is the key to all these products. The design of the stores is very interesting, in which the binary logic of supermarkets is physically reproduced. I use my local supermarket as a typical example to show these relations.

### Layout of Supermarket Periphery

The perimeter of supermarkets is where the high-volume perishables are sold and the inside areas, called in the trade, "the jungle," is where the staples are sold. One of the basic problems for supermarkets is luring people into the jungle and getting them to spend time there, since there is a direct correlation between time spent shopping and money spent by the customer.

When we go to supermarkets we spend time, literally and figuratively. Although there are, in principle, an infinite number of routes that a shopper might take in any given supermarket, I have found (by observing customers at the supermarkets where I buy things on a number of cases, as an example) that people tend to take the same route over and over again. There are two "logical" ways of exploring the supermarket: the *circumference route* in which you circle the periphery of the store and venture into various aisles to find specific things, and the *in-and-out route*, in which you go up and down each aisle you come to and shop in the circumference in passing.

Generally speaking, people take the circumference route, in which they move through the outside areas of the supermarket first, picking up the fruits and vegetables, dairy products, and meat they need—and then venture into the jungle. This gives more continuity than the in-and-out route, starting at one end and going up and down the aisles until the other end is reached. The problem with this route is that it is impossible to cover the circumference as easily as with the first route. People are led, then, to use the circumference route because it is much more convenient and flows much more smoothly. The supermarket is a kind of labyrinth (emotionally speaking) that channels our behavior much more than we might imagine.

Because cuisine is so complicated (and so useful as a way of getting at cultural values), the supermarket is of enormous utility to the student of social relations. The coloration of supermarket walls—with green, white, and red for vegetables, dairy, and meat—and the different oppositions contained in the supermarket, are worth considering. For example, if we take money in its symbolic coloration, we can see it as black (filthy lucre), so that the cash register area symbolically is black, forming the opposite of the dairy area, white.

An examination of the contents of the supermarket is also very revealing, for we find that, generally, cultural priorities are reflected in products sold. Thus, the enormous amount of space devoted to dog and cat food tells us something about the place of pets in American society. (Pet food is something like a $5 or $6 billion a year industry here.) The space devoted to frozen foods and "instant" products tells us something about our attitudes toward time, and toward food itself—or, at least, attitudes in the large numbers of people who use these products.

This chapter has been an examination of the logical structure of supermarkets, seeing them not as simply "stores" but as institutions containing interesting oppositions and polarities. A cuisine may be seen from this perspective as something that mediates between the oppositions in the food supply, just as a supermarket is an institution that mediates between producers of foods and related products and customers.

The supermarket provides a fantastic "show," but at $100 or so a week, a moderate bill for a family of four, it isn't a cheap one. (Relatively speaking, however, Americans spend a much smaller percentage of their income on food than people in most other countries.) There are attempts now, by several companies, to get people to shop for groceries on the Internet. Whether these companies will be successful remains to be seen. At present, only a relatively small percentage of people are using these services but it may be different with a new generation of young people, who have been brought up using computers and who are comfortable with the Internet.

## CODES IN THE CLASSROOM: EXCLUSIVITY ENCOURAGES PASSIVITY

There is a great deal of concern, nowadays, about what goes on in the college classroom. It is useful to examine what goes on in a typical classroom structurally, in terms of who controls what space, who talks and who is talked to, rather than in terms of the content of the material being presented or the personality of the teacher. What we find, when we examine the relationships between professors and students in this manner, is that they are generally placed in oppositional roles and that frequently the very design of the classroom contributes to this. Let us examine the relationships more closely:

| **Professor** | **Students** |
|---|---|
| Stands | Sit |
| Walks around | Remain stationary |
| Looks at everyone | All look at professor |
| (is center of attention) | (givers of attention) |
| Is "higher" physically | Are "lower" physically |
| Active as a rule: acts | Passive as a rule: react |
| Talks | Listen |
| Gives information | Take information |
| Starts and finishes period | Operate in time parameters set by professor |
| Active aggression via sarcasm | Passive aggression via nonresponse, inertness |
| Judges and rewards | Are judged and rewarded |
| Dominant position in organization | Subservient positions in organization |
| Controls media: blackboard | Consume media: blackboard |
| Has territory: front of room | Have territory: rest of room |

Generally speaking, professors stand to deliver their lectures or to lead or attempt to lead discussions, and generally the students sit. I have sketched, in the list just given, typical situations, of course. Not all classes are run this way, but what I have described is fairly typical for the standard lecture or discussion (as contrasted with seminar) course.

Some lecturers grab hold of the lecturn and do not let go for dear life during the period—the lecturn furnishing security and having symbolic significance, but many lecturers stroll around, moving between the lecturn and the blackboard, demonstrating "intimacy," from behind the lecturn to or toward the students. The professor is "high," in that he or she stands and the student is, typically, "low," in that he or she sits.

Given the situation I have sketched out, with its extreme separation of modes of behavior, it is natural for a kind of alienation to exist and for the students to be passive. Passivity is one of the real problems in the classroom no matter what the situation is. If a professor lectures the entire period, the student is automatically placed in a passive state. If the professor leads a discussion and there isn't much talking by the students (as is frequently the case), there is apt to be frustration on both sides. (It may be that a professor leads a discussion and there is a great deal of participation by the students, but we must assume that this is probably an exception to the rule. Otherwise, articles about upgrading teaching would not need to be written.)

Given the structure of authority in an educational institution (or organization, to be more accurate, since colleges and universities are organizations, with rules and policies, and so on), students find it hard to show aggression other than in one way—and that is nonresponse, or what some have called *passive aggression*. Students who do not respond to their teachers are being "aggressive" in a passive rather than an active way, but they are still being aggressive. They adopt this form of aggression because they can be penalized for other forms of aggression and because it is a response they pick up, without even recognizing it, in society at large.

But students are, in subtle ways, encouraged in this passivity by the structural organization of the classroom and its separation of student and teacher by physical as well as other means. The problem is exacerbated by the fact that students have certain expectations that fit within the framework just described. Namely, as I have discovered in occasional efforts to foster peer-group instruction, many students say they are paying money to be taught by somebody who "knows what he is talking about," has advanced degrees, and so on, and they resent it when I try to escape from the typical teacher–student relationship.

They see discussions as an attempt to shirk my responsibilities because they have defined the classroom experience in terms of the traditional broadcasting and receiving relationship. They like the passive stance because it does not threaten their egos and because they are used to taking notes and doing little else. Taking notes from this point of view is a kind of pseudo-activity; they soothe their egos by writing things down, but they do not actually get involved in classroom activities. The tension between boredom and risk is almost always resolved in favor of boredom.

There are a number of economic factors that make it necessary to rely on the lecture format in many situations; lecturing is probably the cheapest way to deliver large amounts of information to a big audience. What is tragic is when smaller classes are conducted like large lectures because the professors and the students cannot find a way to deal with the codes that exist for each. These codes confine each of the participants and destroy what should be an exciting and rewarding experience for both.

Students are, too often, bored and alienated, and it is only the threat of failing examinations that motivates them to study. Teachers are "drained" of life, and instead of finding teaching rewarding and stimulating, discover that the steady diet of passive aggression or aggressive passivity makes teaching often a kind of mild torture.

I have talked about teachers and students in rather extreme ways here, in order to make relations clear. Frequently, of course, things are not as black as this and many students and teachers find their courses exciting and pleasurable. But too often the destructive codes dominate; when students and professors are forced into their niches, the experience for each tends to be disappointing, if not destructive!

We face new problems with the development of the Internet and "distance" learning. The classroom codes do not operate but other codes do, and the passive student now becomes a "lurker" who contributes as little as possible to online discussions. All human relationships have difficulties and one of the most difficult is that of the professor who "judges" and the student who "is judged."

# Chapter 8

# *The Agent in the Agency*

*NOTE: This ethnography relates my "adventures" and experiences during a 3-week stay at Goldberg Moser O'Neill (GMO), a large San Francisco advertising agency (where I was a visiting professor thanks to the Advertising Educational Foundation) and a visit in 1973 at a large British advertising agency, where I spent a few weeks wandering around and observing what was going on. I spent 1973 in London on sabbatical, doing research on British popular culture, and my stay at the agency was part of that research. A friend of mine who worked in an American ad agency knew the creative director of a British agency, and as a result of a letter my friend wrote, I was able to spend some time at the British agency. I was housed in the creative director's office and was free to do whatever I wanted during my visit there.*

*I wrote an ethnography, titled* The UK *(a play on words about a famous tribe, the Ik) about my experiences in London that contained this material on the British advertising agency as well as analyses of British humor, food, television, and numerous aspects of everyday life. I found the people who worked at the British agency extremely well educated, intelligent, and very hospitable. If I have any generalizations to make about people who work in advertising, based on my experiences at the two agencies, it is that they tend to be very bright and hard working, but also they are often frustrated by having to deal with clients who lack imagination and daring.*

*I found a remarkable similarity in outlook between the people I spent time with in Britain in 1973 and in San Francisco in 1999, which may be because trying to sell things to people hasn't changed that much over the past 40 or 50 years. I also found that the impact of British advertising methods was considerable at GMO, which employed a number of people from the United Kingdom.*

\* \* \* \* \*

My adventure at GMO started in early April 1999 when I received an e-mail message from the Advertising Education Foundation in New York indicating that they had selected me to participate in its Visiting Professor program. I was astounded because I had written mostly negative articles about advertising and I was well over the age of most people who participate in the program. That message led to my getting in touch with Catrina McAuliffe, senior vice president and chief marketing officer at GMO, who took me to lunch, along with the agency's public relations manager, Ruth Grossman.

We went to an Italian restaurant near the agency. The waiters got all mixed up about our orders, it seems, and it took a long time for us to get served. While we waited we chatted about advertising and what I might do at the agency.

## Catrina McAuliffe

Catrina is an Englishwoman with a long background in advertising. She's been with GMO since before it started in 1990, I believe. Originally, GMO was the San Francisco branch of Chiat/Day (GMO bought out Chiat/Day). One of the first things she said to me, at the restaurant (Faz) was "the days of three martini lunches are over. Goldberg Moser O'Neill is a lean and mean machine."

A bit later Catrina asked me "What do you want us to do for you, and what can you do for us?"

I had prepared a sheet in which I listed some things I hoped to learn at the agency and I also indicated some things I might do for the agency.

"I can keep quiet at any meeting I might go to," I said, "or I can participate in any meetings I might attend . . . whatever you want. And also, I can offer some workshops for the people at GMO."

I had brought along a list of some comedy writing workshops I had given. I also gave her a copy of a comic mystery I had written called *The Hamlet Case*, and a copy of my comic murder mystery/textbook, *Postmortem for a Postmodernist*, to give her an idea of my writing style.

"My son told me not to be zany," I said.

"We like zany people," she replied.

I felt rather strange having to "market" myself to an experienced marketer, I must admit. But I tried to be honest and explain why I wanted to visit GMO and what I could do for them.

"You don't fit the usual profile," she said.

"I've heard that before," I replied.

That was in mid-April. We corresponded by e-mail over the next couple of weeks and we finally agreed to have me start on May 10, 1999. I had sent various lists of workshops I could offer, and everything was set for me to start on May 10.

## First Day at the Agency

On May 10 I arrived at GMO at 9:30 a.m. and was given a tour of the agency by Barbara Brennan, Catrina's executive assistant. Barbara came to GMO originally as a temp and decided she liked advertising and the people at GMO liked her. She had a background in computers and after that studied at a culinary academy and worked for a number of years as a chef.

"I ran a restaurant," she told me.

The office they gave me is just down the aisle from Fred Goldberg, who seems to be the numero uno in the agency. Later on during the day I bumped into him and we shook hands.

"Thanks for inviting me. I'm having a wonderful time, so far."

He replied, "Well, you might not be so happy by the time you're through here."

I found that comment a bit strange. People I met at the agency had told me "Fred's bark is worse than his bite."

Someone at the agency had a sign made with my name on it, which was placed outside my cubicle. I also found a box with stationery supplies in it. I also had a GMO sweatshirt—extra large size, a Kia tee shirt, and a GMO baseball cap with "No Shit" embroidered on the front. Various people came in to help me put my name in the phone service and get my computer set. Then I had a meeting at 10 a.m. with Yvonne Yarnold, another Englishwoman. She's a VP and a group account director.

## Yvonne Yarnold

I had written about print advertisements and commercials in the past . . . but always as an interpreter or critic looking at the final product . . . and trying to figure out how the ad generated meaning, what effects it might have had on people, and what it reflected about society and culture. Yvonne offered an interesting analogy: "You can think of me as being like an architect," she said. "I help translate the desires of the person who wants to have a house built into a plan for a house that works." Her job, as I understand things, involves helping clients determine what they really want or, in some cases, finding out what would be best for them. This is done by developing a creative brief, which takes the desires and needs of the client into account and describes what the advertising will do. She explained that there are three disciplines involved when dealing with clients:

> The Brand Planner at the agency thinks "my consumer." The Creative People in the agency think "my creation" (the ad or commercial). The Account People of the agency think "my brand."

What has to be done, she suggested, is to create an impression about the brand in the minds and hearts of people . . . create a personality for the product by giving it attributes, a personality . . . using copy, art, photographs, and carrying that personality through all marketing communications vehicles, such as the logo and packaging.

There was a lot of concern at GMO about redefining itself as an agency noted for its creativity. I don't know what its reputation was earlier, but I had read a description of it on the Internet as a "good Grade B agency." That would suggest a certain level of competence but not brilliance. I imagine that GMO wanted to redefine itself with Goodby, Silverstein—perhaps the "hottest" agency in San Francisco—in mind. Someone told me that GMO had a regional reputation for being creative but it wanted to get national recognition.

The people at GMO tend to talk about brands all the time, rather than products. I guess that advertising is involved, in the final analysis, with *branding* people—a term that has interesting connotations because we also think of branding as applying red hot metal brands (with the name of a ranch) to the sides of steers. Is there a similar kind of process at work in advertising, except that instead of using red-hot brands, advertisements and commercials are used? The important thing is that a powerful impression has been made on the consumer—one that lasts and, to keep to the steer-branding metaphor, says "one of ours." This kind of branding is done when the consumer identifies with some brand of product.

But how does this identification work? That is one of the things I was trying to find out during my stay at GMO. I was not sure how to go about making sense of GMO . . . there were 275 people working there. It was originally an agency with 60 people . . . so it had grown enormously. I decided to see what I could learn from chatting with people and maybe even taking part in some discussions.

I was in the middle of chatting with Yvonne when someone came and said she was needed at a meeting, so she had to rush off.

"This happens all the time," she said.

I can believe that. I know that Catrina seemed to spend her life racing from meeting to meeting. At the time of my visit, GMO had Dreyer's Grand Ice Cream for an account, and Dreyer's had a case full of ice cream in a kitchen upstairs where there was coffee, some chairs and tables, and a refrigerator. I had already had some ice cream, but was determined to not succumb to the temptation too often.

## Dennis O'Rourke

Dennis O'Rourke, the chief financial officer, popped in to introduce himself. I hoped to chat with him a bit. I wanted to find out how many people at GMO were copywriters and artists, how many were account executives, how many were accountants, and that kind of thing. I imagined that advertising agencies were like icebergs with a small number of creative people at the top and a huge mass of other supporting people beneath them. But I may have been mistaken.

I wonder whether most of the big agencies can put on creative and imaginative commercials if they have the right clients or whether some agencies just don't have the creative talent? One thing I learned is that the clients generally play a much bigger role in things than I had imagined they did. Not always, of course. I also wonder to what degree the creative people are "guided" by the "creative brief"?

I say this because creative people I know tend to do whatever they want to do, tend to be "laws unto themselves." So I find it hard to imagine that some of the people who actually create the commercials give a damn about what the marketers have found and the briefs that the account executives and brand planners and account managers and media people and all the other layers of noncreatives draw up for them.

Someone I know who was in advertising said agencies can best be described as "organized chaos." I didn't get that sense at GMO, but I didn't have much of a sense yet of what goes on there because I had only been there a few hours. There were people at GMO who seemed to be making frantic phone calls and running back and forth. Maybe that was the chaos? Or maybe there was something else? If so, I hoped to find out what it was.

## Jeff Shubert

Jeff Shubert is an account director who is involved with the Cisco Systems commercials—which I think have been an enormous success since they started running, and done a great deal for Cisco System's image of itself and for the GMO sense of itself as a creative agency. He said the Cisco Systems commercials have done a number of things: First, they increased awareness of the Cisco brand among corporate decision makers; second, they "moved the needle" as far as informing people about Cisco's key role in building the Internet; third, they improved Cisco's image attributes and last, but not least, they were tremendously motivating and inspiring to Cisco's employees.

The company is now perceived as global in nature, friendly (maybe even compassionate), and one that people should want to do business with. Cisco Systems is an enormous company, but until the campaign, it was relatively obscure, as far as awareness by the general public is concerned. Now, Cisco Systems has been given a great deal of visibility and an image of being humane in a world of technology that tends to be rather cold and sterile. This was done by focusing on people rather than technology and gizmos in the commercials.

The commercials have been an enormous success and have helped the Cisco sales force, as it competes with other technology companies. According to Shubert, the strategy for the commercials was based on three pillars: *humanity* (it has a warm image), *substance* (truthful statements about Cisco's role and how the Internet is changing the world), and *urgency* (the need for companies to take advantage of the Internet or be left behind). One message implied in the campaign is that fast companies that use the Internet and the latest technology, beat slow companies.

The GMO strategy, he explained, was to establish Cisco Systems as a brand, reflect the culture of the company, differentiate Cisco Systems from other technology companies, and give the Internet a "human" image. The commercials took about 6 months, from the time GMO got the assignment until the time they were shot. In 1999, GMO was using the popularity of the commercials in print campaigns. The commercials seemed to have had an enormous impact on the sales force at Cisco Systems. An Internet service provider customer of Cisco Systems told an executive of the company "the commercials made me feel good about the business I'm in." The campaign also gave a boost to GMO's image as it re-defined itself nationally as a "creative" agency. One client of GMO said to an executive of the agency, "I didn't realize you could do that kind of work." GMO was described, in one article I read on the Internet, as a "good Grade B advertising agency." However, in the April 19, 1999 issue of *Adweek Magazine,* GMO was given an "A minus" rating when evaluated against nine other Western U.S.-based agencies. Only one other agency received the same rating. All the rest received grades of "Bs" and "Cs."

Every once in a while, and it is hard to figure out exactly how it happens, a commercial is made that has enormous resonance with the public. The Macintosh "1984" commercial is one of the best examples of this kind of thing. It seems that the Cisco campaign also struck a chord and had an impact beyond the wildest dreams of GMO and Cisco Systems. Unlike the "1984" commercial, which portrayed a dehumanized totalitarian society, the Cisco Systems campaign stressed the role technology can play in bringing people together and in affirming the importance of all people. Coincidentally, both were done by the same agency, as GMO grew out of Chiat/Day San Francisco—the agency responsible for "1984."

"Are you ready?" the Cisco commercials asked?

Cisco Systems expected to hear that thanks to its technology, the answer is "yes."

It so happens that Fred Goldberg, the chairman and chief executive officer of GMO, was at Chiat/Day when the 1984 commercial was made. He was instrumental in getting it aired, because Apple didn't want to run it during the 1984 Super Bowl. Apple had purchased two spots for commercials. Goldberg managed to sell one of them, but he dragged his feet on selling the second, so Apple was more or less forced to run the "1984" commercial—probably the most famous commercial ever made.

Goldberg showed me some research that indicated that a focus group that had seen the commercial before it ran gave it a very poor rating. It was given a "5," whereas the ordinary commercial gets a "30" or "35" rating by focus groups. As Goldberg pointed out in a presentation he gave at Stanford, research tends to lead to conservative advertising. So, my visit to GMO provided me with an interesting insight into the "1984" commercial and into the tensions that exist in advertising between the counters (number crunchers) and the creatives in advertising agencies. Art directors and copywriters are called "creatives" by everyone in the agency.

## Gaynor Strachan Chun

Gaynor Strachan Chun is one of seven account directors at GMO. She is also one of eight female vice presidents at the agency. She explained to me the hierarchy that exists in the Account Management Department at the agency. At the senior level are the account directors, who may handle a number of different accounts. Working with them are management supervisors, account supervisors and account executives, each with their own responsibilities, but essentially involved day to day with the clients and ultimately the campaigns being developed. The entry-level position is assistant account executive who is responsible for billing and all kinds of other "grunt" work. (Informally, account people in advertising agencies are often called "suits.") The Account Management Department has a total staff of more than 60 people. There are around 30 art directors and copywriters in the Creative Department, and the rest of the agency is made up of everything from brand planners to accountants to media planners to production artists.

The account directors work closely with all departments within the agency. However, one of the critical roles they play is to work with the brand planners to determine the objectives and strategy for the advertising campaigns. Brand planners focus on the "man and woman in the street," the customers for the products or the services that are being advertised. They are responsible for uncovering consumer insights that will help the advertising be more compelling to the target at hand. Account management is responsible for understanding the client's business, the issues they face and ensuring the advertising is compelling from a business perspective. They are also responsible for the relationship with the client.

I asked her for a case study that would show her contributions to a campaign, and she gave me the example of Citra.

### A Case Study: Citra

The Coca-Cola Company is one of GMO's clients. GMO handles Citra, one of The Coca-Cola Company's products. Dealing with Coca-Cola is complicated because it has many different policies and guidelines that have to be followed, so it is challenging to maneuver under these conditions. Coca-Cola has 150 products around the world, all beverages, and so it is natural that it would develop certain policies and strategies for its agencies to follow. Nevertheless, Coca-Cola believes in the power of advertising and is willing to re-look at the rules should a compelling argument be delivered. In the case of the Citra campaign, GMO had presented two versions of the same campaign. They believed that one of the versions (all black and white) was far more compelling, both for the brand and the consumer. However, the recommended campaign did not include some of the executional elements that Coca-Cola felt were important to include. GMO and Coca-Cola agreed to elicit some consumer input to resolve the issue. Focus groups among the core target were conducted with both the client and members of the GMO team in attendance. As a result of attending the focus groups and hearing the consumer responses to the campaigns, it was agreed that the all black-and-white campaign was more compelling and would have a stronger impact in the marketplace. This was a joint decision that was made possible due to the partnership that had developed between the client and the agency. The GMO campaign positions Citra as "the ultimate thirst eliminating soda." "No thirst is safe," the Citra commercials tell us because Citra "assassinates" thirst gangsters. There are currently two commercials in the campaign: "Washed up Gangster" and "Raid." They are both very funny.

"How do commercials like the ones you did sell soda pop?" I asked. Like so many things about advertising, it is hard to answer that question. That's because we can never be sure how advertising works in any particular case. The answer I got from talking with people at GMO is that if people notice the commercial, connect with the message and therefore the product being advertised at an emotional level and like the advertising, they are more likely to try Citra. However, as with all forms of communication, they don't work in isolation of each other. Especially with the youth market that Coca-Cola brands are targeting. Carbonated soft drinks are predominantly "sold" on the strength of the image they portray and whether or not the target thinks that image is "cool."

**Paul Carek**

Paul is a copywriter who worked on the Citra account.

"Coke targeted its commercials at 14- to 16-year-old kids . . . it wanted us to send a message saying 'this it the best soda to drink when you're having a good time with your friends.' But we wanted to do something different. We wanted to come up with an unusual approach, to get Citra noticed."

"We hit on the concept 'No thirst is safe' and then we personified thirst using film noir. Kids don't have to see kids on the screen to know soda is to be drunk. We made two commercials—one in color with traditional shots of kids enjoying the soda that included a segment in black and white, and one all in black and white, and the kids liked the all black-and-white commercials the best."

"Who does Citra compete with?" I asked. I'd never heard of the drink before.

"Citra is fighting for recognition among grapefruit-based drinks. We like to think of our ads as Squirt killers. We dramatized the benefit—their thirst being in danger. The game is trying to get kids to try it once. If they do, our research indicates that they'll drink it again."

"How did you think up the idea of having a gangster and using film noir?" I asked.

He smiled. "We were sitting in a bar in Seattle talking about the account and the idea suddenly came to us. Usually, when we have a brief, we brainstorm for a few days. We have to work through the 'hack' stage—the ideas that everyone thinks of, the conventional ideas. We're searching for originality."

It all seemed quite remarkable to me. Ideas seem to pop into the heads of the creatives—the copywriters and art directors—after they have struggled with the problem of what to do. That seems to be the way creativity works. Somehow, out of the blue, an idea comes into someone's head. Then, that idea has become a commercial.

## Dave Doyle

I had an appointment at 10 a.m. with Dave Doyle, an account director, but he cancelled it at the last minute, so I was scouting around, looking for people to chat with . . . especially in the creative side of the agency. I called Mike Moser's secretary and made an appointment for the following week. He had a big pitch coming up, and I assumed he wanted to be able to spend all his time working on it.

## Chuck Meehan and Matt Mowat

I went down to the fifth floor and had a chat with Chuck Meehan, a copywriter, and Matt Mowat, an art director—they work as a team. They had just won an award in New York for some commercials they did and were in a good mood. I assume that all the creative teams are made up the same way. They were dressed very casually . . . one wore a t-shirt and jeans, and they were very friendly. I got some interesting insights into the business from talking with them.

"These awards are important," Chuck said. "There's a lot of competition internally," he said. "All the teams here want to do well. So getting an award gives a person status in the advertising world."

I suspect that winning an award also means you can expect a big boost in your salary because agencies are always scouting around for new talent, for "stars."

I asked him how they worked.

"We try to make ads that evoke an emotion . . . humor is often useful in this respect. We brainstorm together about ideas that might be used for an ad. Usually we come up with three or four ideas for a spot. Then others here get involved, and we usually choose one of these ideas for the spot. We're looking for the single most compelling idea to communicate!"

"It seems to me like what I used to do when I was a counselor at summer camps," I said. "A few of us would get together and think up a skit to do and then we'd put it on."

"You've got to realize," Matt said, "we never own an account. They come and go. We have them for a while . . . and try to do the best we can. But new business is the life of an agency."

## Dave Doyle

I got to talk with Dave Doyle at 1:30 p.m. He had been called away that morning, at the last minute, to give a talk at an advertising club meeting . . . substituting for someone else who couldn't make it. Dave is an account director who handles the Kia Motors America account.

"We try to make our advertising distinctive," he said, "to generate an awareness factor in people . . . to get their attention. We do this by doing ads that are irreverent and quirky. Our ads aren't of cars racing down highways. We also point out the price differentials between Kias and other cars. They're a couple of thousand dollars cheaper than the models they compete with."

"Kia works hard to keep their dealers happy and to maximize their profitability. A Kia franchise doesn't cost much and Kia shares advertising costs with its dealers. So the dealers put some energy into selling Kias."

"I looked up the Kias in *Consumer Reports*," I said. "They didn't get good reviews. In fact, the reviews were terrible."

Dave shrugged his shoulders. "We have to deal with a different mindset among the Korean car manufacturers . . . but they are changing. They used to think the big thing was to make a big margin on each sale, but they've found that warranty claims against the cars are costing them a fortune. The Korean economy also tanked, and that deprived them of the money they need to make their cars better."

He suggested, as we talked, that the Kia people were aware of this problem and were going to do something about it.

"When we run Kia ads, people come into their showrooms," he said. "Kia has boosted it sales considerably over the past few years. Kia sold 55,000 cars 3 years ago. Last year, Kia sold 82,000 cars and for 1999 the target is 115,000 cars." The people at GMO talked a good deal about tracking. By this they mean increasing awareness of Kia as well as consideration of Kia among persons who are in a car-buying frame of mind. It may mean increased traffic in the showroom, but the real goal is making headway among "intenders."

I asked him why people would buy Kias when there are Japanese cars like Hondas and Toyotas that are so reliable.

"Buyers of Kias can be characterized by a couple of things. They're willing to risk money on a vehicle that they perceive as 'different,' and they need to get a new car . . . their old car may have broken down. They want to get a brand new car and they don't want to pay very much for it. So they're willing to give Kia a try. People can get a new Kia for just under $10,000."

"We market the car by suggesting it has Japanese-like quality but costs less. That's the message we want to give people."

"You're using a halo effect. Japanese quality is the halo," I said, "and Kia is trying to get some of the glow from the halo."

"Kia can be seen as an immigrant who comes to the United States. It has five qualities . . . what we call the '5 Hs'—Kias are hardworking, humble, human, honest, and with a sense of humor. It's an un-Detroit car. Most car companies bludgeon people, hitting them over and over again with their ads. Kia's account is only $100 million."

"A hundred million dollars seems like quite a bit of money," I said.

"You've got realize that we spend $12 billion annually on car advertising in America," he said. "So $100 million isn't very much. We produce 4 to 6 national television spots, 4 spots for national sales events, 15 newspaper ads, and 10 radio commercials in a typical year. We also create an ad planner that we ship to dealers and banners for their showrooms."

After I left Dave, I started doing some calculating. If we spend $12 billion a year on advertising for cars and we sell 15 millions cars and trucks (give or take a million or two), we're spending quite a bit of money on advertising for each car. It adds up to around $800 for advertising for each car.

## The Goldberg Moser O'Neill Reel

I had seen the GMO reel one night . . . they send it to potential clients to give them an idea about what kind of advertising they do . . . and found it quite interesting. Some of the commercials were quite clever . . . lots of humor in the commercials and some remarkable visuals. I couldn't help but wonder, as I watched the reel, about the enormous amount of effort that went into them . . . hundreds of thousand of dollars for 15 or 30 seconds (one commercial cost around $500,000 to make), dozens of people involved in research, thinking up the ideas for the commercials and then creating them . . . and what do you have—a 15- or 30-second (or at the most, a 60-second) mini-drama on videotape or celluloid.

Of course that mini-drama will be on television and millions of people will probably see it, and it might possibly affect their decisions (and if not them, someone else's decisions) about what soft drink to buy the next day or what jeans to wear or where to go for a vacation or what car to buy. The advertising industry is enormous; we spend around $250 billion a year on advertising in America and the businesses that hire advertising agencies use them, obviously, because they produce results.

**Kim Ball**

I spoke with Kim Ball . . . an account director who has three accounts: Quantum, carclub.com, Inc. (an Internet company), and the Monterey Bay Aquarium. She struck me as a very self-possessed young woman . . . who was a bit anxious to get back to her work and probably wondered what I was doing at GMO and why I was talking with her.

She started describing her position, and I asked her a question about the difference between account directors and account executives.

"Don't you know anything about advertising agencies?" she asked.

I explained to her what I was doing at GMO. "I'm not interested, to any great extent, in the organizational structure of the agency and in all the various layers of account supervisors and account managers and account executives who are floating around," I said. "I do want to learn what all the different people do, but primarily I'm interested in how a print advertisement or a commercial moves from conceptualization to actualization. What goes into making a 30-second or 60-second commercial?"

I asked her about her background because I was curious about how people end up in advertising. "I was an English major at UCLA," she said. She started as a temporary employee at Ogilvy & Mather, then got a position as an assistant account executive, and this led, eventually, to her taking a position at GMO. "There's more collaboration between people at this agency than at many others," she said. I took it that collaboration is something she felt was very positive.

"Quantum wants to generate two ideas with its advertising: reliability and protection. The Quantum advertisements do this," she explained, "by using metaphors to generate these ideas."

Advertising agencies search for "universal metaphors" that people everywhere in the universe—or at least people in Quantum's target audience—will be able to understand easily. Account Managers, among other things, are involved in developing a creative brief—it tells the target audience the compelling reason why they should subscribe to the brand or product. As she put it, "if we could say one single, compelling, differentiating reason to believe in this brand or product, what would we say?" The account managers develop this brief, so I understand, by looking at what the companies they are competing with are doing in their advertisements and by figuring out what is unique or special about their brand or message.

"We have to understand the competitive landscape of our client's business," she said. "We're involved in day-to-day relationships with our clients, which means our clients expect us to know as much or more about their marketplace than they do."

I checked over the organizational chart of the agency and discovered that there were more than 50 account managers of one sort or another. There are account executives, account supervisors, management supervisors, account directors, account coordinators, group account directors, and so on. Advertising agencies are, it turns out, very structured. With nearly 25 accounts and most everyone assigned to more than one, they have to be.

## Nancy Hill

My first interview, with Nancy Hill, at 10 a.m. did not come off because she was called to a meeting. So I had a bit of time to write up my notes from the previous day and speculate about this and that. So I did some writing. Nancy is in charge of getting new business. She popped in later to say that she hoped to get together with me in the near future.

My second interview of the day, with an art director named Dave Woodside, at 11 a.m. was cancelled because of some emergency that came up. So I did some more writing. My third interview with Grant Johnson, at 12:30 was also cancelled. So I did some more writing.

The people at this agency seemed to be ferociously busy. And various deadlines and emergencies kept coming up, so I could never count on any meeting that had been arranged for me coming off. I always assumed that any meeting that had been set up for me might be cancelled, for one reason or another. Once I realized that was the case, I found it much easier to negotiate my stay at GMO.

I found, also, that I got into discussions with people informally. I was talking with one of the senior people in the duplicating room. "I don't have time to think," she said. "At any moment any one of five or six people can pop in and distract me, and sometimes they come one after the other so I have to do my thinking out of the shop."

## Andrew Clarke

Andrew Clarke is an Englishman who studied marketing at Lancaster University and is involved in brand planning.

"I could have studied literature at Oxford but chose marketing at Lancaster," he said, with a look on his face that suggested he realized, too late, that he might have made a big mistake. He eventually got a job at Ogilvy & Mather (O&M) as a production assistant.

"At O&M I was at the bottom of the ladder," he said. "Advertising is not a career," he added, "But a way of life. After half a dozen years you have to make a decision—either to get out or to devote your life to it."

I told him that I was astonished at the amount of work people in advertising do, putting in long hours, coming in weekends . . . that sort of thing. He explained to me that he's a brand planner, a position that was invented in British advertising agencies. "We give support to the consumer to counter the junk that comes from corporate marketing departments. You can think of us as bullshit detectors for the client, the agency and sometimes ourselves. We portray the consumer as he relates to the brand. We interpret the consumer's responses to the stimuli he is exposed to—both strategic ideas and potential advertising—and use that information to inform creative judgment as well as to influence broader marketing activities. Account Executives are shock absorbers . . . they cushion the blows from the client's marketing people to the agency and vice versa. Their most important skill is often political; it involves making friends with the corporate marketing people and the agency staff, often teaching clients something about how their product should be marketed and managing the agency's egos. They have to mediate between the forces that can set irrelevant agendas, namely some creative peoples' desires to just be creative and some clients' desires to do the safest thing, forcing a compromise between the agency and client."

"It doesn't sound like too much fun," I replied.

"Remember what Churchill said about advertising agencies—they represent 'The greatest waste of human intelligence outside of chess.' But people in advertising agencies really care about what they do. There's a great deal of energy, passion and sweat involved in making advertisements and commercials."

"Advertising is for *drama queens*," he continued. "The psychological profile for people in advertising is that of people who love the drama involved in working in agencies and the excitement generated by making ads and commercials. Also, planning is about demonstrating that it's not just about logic. It's not a linear process. In the United States, business people are rewarded for being extremely logical . . . and having statistics to back themselves up. This produces dreadful advertising that often fails to make any impact. Advertising agencies are refuges for people who don't only think in a linear fashion and who recognize that people—consumers of advertising—don't think that way, either."

I asked, "How do the people advertising agencies target think and how do advertising agencies reach them?"

"Depends on the people and the brand and the category. For example, in pleasure categories, we can identify known drivers of behavior. There are some known behavioral levers to pull: sex, social identification, that kind of thing. Most often you have an instinct for what is really going on, what really drives people, in a given situation. In some businesses, they articulate these motivators in things like benefit ladders."

"What's benefit laddering?" I asked.

"This term refers to the connections that are made by advertisers between the emotional benefits, rational benefits, and attributes of the product," he replied.

"Package goods marketers love this kind of thing. Take wine, for example. There are red wine brands that position themselves as strong, for tough male aggressor characters. They push the wine's strong taste and offer, as a possible attribute, something like it being grown on mountains that might suggest ruggedness and strength. Whether you subscribe to this or not, in any decision there's an emotional element and this is the lever that advertising can often pull most effectively. And consumers are increasingly sophisticated; it takes more than a vacuous promise and a pretty face to get advertising-savvy consumers to buy these days."

I found my interview with Andrew quite interesting. Advertising is, as he saw it, full of drama queens . . . and drama kings, as well.

**Mary Beth Gilliam**

Mary Beth Gilliam was in meetings from 8:30 a.m. until 12:30 p.m. Right after her 12:30 p.m. meeting she came to chat with me at my cubicle . . . she hadn't had a moment for lunch. Like many others, she'd had an internship in advertising and decided to make it a career. She had been the advertising director of her college newspaper and made a lot of money at it and that had also fueled a desire in her for advertising. She had more than 10 years of experience in the advertising business.

She is also a brand planner.

"Clients come to advertising agencies because they often can't see the forest for the trees. Many clients don't understand who or what they are and we have to help them discover their identities. Brand planners foster a close relation with their clients and with the creatives in the agency. We want the creatives to have some ideas to create from."

We talked about how agencies are graded.

"I looked up GMO on the Internet, when I found out that I was going to be coming here, and one article described it as a good Grade B agency," I said.

"There are only a couple of agencies that everyone would agree are 'A' agencies: Goodby and TWBA/Chiat/Day. Others would add W&K [Wieden and Kennedy]," she replied. "But we're a creative agency and we'd like to become an 'A' agency."

"On my second day on the job," she continued, "we had a focus group for Dreyer's ice cream. It was full of mothers with children in their households and dealt with how they used ice cream. We discovered that there are very few things you do with kids, when they are young, that they don't grow out of. One activity is skiing and another is eating ice cream. It has the remarkable power to facilitate communication between people. It is enjoyable and it reminds people of their childhoods. So we decided to align Dreyer's with what we called 'family moments' and worked on developing a campaign using Dreyer's as a catalyst for bonding children and their parents and for bonding Dreyer's with consumers of ice cream."

I had recalled one amusing Dreyer's commercial that GMO produced. An elderly lady is walking down the street when her container of Dreyer's falls on the ground and rolls under a car. She can't reach it, so she lifts the car up on its side and nudges the container of Dreyer's over with her foot, until she can get it. I thought it was a very clever commercial that relied on humor to make its point. I wondered how an agency could ever produce data to prove that a proposed campaign would be effective . . . because advertising is an art form and art and statistics don't fit together very well.

## Patti Young

Patti Young is a brand planner who worked on the Boston Market account for GMO for 1 year, developing a new strategy for Boston Market to use. But after Boston Market implemented the strategy on a regional basis, it went bankrupt.

"I'm one of Catrina's crew," she said. "We represent the consumer at the agency and work with the creatives on the ad campaigns. We want to know how the consumers perceive the brands and how to reach them."

I asked her to give me a case history of the Boston market campaign she worked on, so I could see how brand managers work.

"We did focus groups on moms [she talks about "moms" and "kids"] to see how they view fast food restaurants. Boston Market was a hybrid . . . a fast food restaurant that passed itself off as a casual restaurant, like Chili's or Olive Garden . . . casual restaurants have servers who come to your table."

"As a result of our focus groups, we learned some interesting things about moms and their attitudes toward Boston Market. Fast food restaurants like McDonald's are fast and easy and the kids like the food there. The ones that appeal to kids often have toy giveaways. The mothers liked the idea of getting toys for their kids but also got annoyed, because with every new film, it seems, the fast food restaurants had new toys and the mothers felt they were more or less forced to bring their kids to the restaurants. The mothers liked Boston Market but the kids didn't. That's because Boston Market had no finger foods for the kids and no toys, which bring kids into fast food restaurants. Many of the fast food restaurants also have playgrounds that kids love."

I asked her what GMO did for Boston Market. I could see the problem—Boston Market lacked an identity; it occupied a no-man's land between being a fast food restaurant and a casual one and ended up, so it seems, satisfying neither the customer who was looking for a fast food meal or for a casual meal.

"We put together a few options for Boston Market," Patti said. "We wanted to suggest that Boston Market represented quality food and quality entertainment and come up with toys that were fun and also educational. We played around with a few ideas. One was Fun 101, which had an icon that resembled a college logo and suggested the educational aspects of our toys. The second was Digs, an animal icon that kids in focus groups really liked. And the third was something we called the 'magical backyard.'"

"In addition, we suggested that Boston Market develop kids meals. It had chicken fingers and Jell-O jigglers. Kids drive family eating and push them to go to McDonald's; parents go to places like McDonald's because they know their kids will eat the food there. Our idea, once we went with Digs, was to find toys that the moms liked. We wanted to find interactive give-aways that kids would spend some time with. With most toys, the kids play with them for a few minutes and then forget about them. We had in mind toys such as little binoculars that actually worked, barometers that told the temperature, and a hip canteen. We did focus groups with the kids to try out the toys."

"So what happened?" I asked. "Why did Boston Market go bankrupt?"

"There were a couple of problems that Boston Market couldn't overcome. First, its prices were higher than other fast food restaurants. It is a fast food restaurant but its prices are those charged by casual restaurants. And second, the type of food that Boston Market served was construed by people as holiday fare . . . turkey, chicken, meat loaf. These meals have a holiday image and not an everyday food image. So, although many people go to fast food restaurants once a week, people went to Boston Market on an average of once every 45 days. It's kids' meals that drive frequency. Also, Boston Market was getting mostly adults, not families . . . with lots of kids."

"We came up with a campaign idea—Don't Mess With Dinner—which targeted working moms. They could come to Boston Market and take out the food, so they wouldn't have to cook that night. The problem with Boston Market is that they didn't have anything for kids and by the time we figured out what they could do to solve this problem, it was too late."

## More on Ice Cream and the Dreyer's Account

I went to a weekly staff meeting, held every Monday morning, and discovered that GMO had lost the Dreyer's account. They lost this account, so people at GMO told me, because Dreyer's had hired a consultant who told them the GMO campaign wasn't right for Dreyer's.

The consultant the Dreyer's hired was Jack Stout, one of the authors of *Positioning: The Battle for Your Mind*, which is the Bible for many people in advertising. It was Stout who told Dreyer's that it should have a leadership position. But the problem, as Patti Young explained it to me, is that Dreyer's premium is no different, really, from other premiums like Breyer's or Safeway Select.

"Dreyer's went to Goodby," she said. "They had been doing advertising for Dreyer's super premium brand, Portofino."

"It's vanilla that's the key to ice cream sales," she added. "Some are more icy than others, some are creamier than others . . . and ice cream manufacturers often have a number of different kinds of vanilla—regular vanilla, French vanilla, sugar-free vanilla . . . vanilla is the number one flavor for ice cream brands. Dreyer's has special flavors, but nothing else. In order for Dreyer's to take a leadership position, it would have to change its ice cream. What it has going for it is nostalgia here in the West Coast, where it's been around a long time . . . and a healthy image, too."

These discussions of ice cream and fast foods were, to me, enormously interesting.

## Terry Rietta

Terry is an art director who told me about his work with a copywriter on a series of print ads for Boston Market.

"We had a super speed drill," he said. "We got the assignment on Thursday night for an ad that was to run on Monday morning in newspapers in Charlotte, North Carolina. Boston Market was opening a large gourmet grocery superstore in Charlotte and we had to come up with some ads to tell people about it. My partner, Paul Carek, who's a copywriter, and I didn't get a brief. We were just given the facts and had to come up with a strategy."

"We started brainstorming . . . looking for ideas. We thought of a number of them. The first was 'You could go there every night because they had so many different meals.' That led us to think of another idea—'you'll never have to cook again.' This, in turn, suggested another idea, 'All this stuff in your kitchen is now junk (because it is no longer needed)' which suggested 'what will you do with that stuff—your colanders, pots, etc.'"

"We had certain limitations, too," he added. "We could only use type and line art, because we didn't have a big budget. And we were to make a series of five ads, to run in different parts of newspapers—one in sports, one in a food section . . . that kind of thing. We used our restrictions as a source of ideas. We discovered that lots of people, who presumably had read the ads, checked out the store. There was also the serial nature of the ads. People who had seen one of them wondered what the next ones would be like . . . and looked for them."

"Why is so much advertising bad?" I asked.

"There are a couple of reasons," he said. "First, advertising is hard to do. It's not easy to come up with good commercials and advertisements. In addition, there's the second filter—the clients. They think of themselves and often want to present themselves as something they're not."

"I've heard," I said, "that clients are often a big problem . . . they have conservative tastes and prevent agencies from doing the kinds of ads they're capable to doing if left alone."

"Just go into most homes and look how they're decorated," he said. "They look lousy, because most people have lousy taste," he said. "Let me explain why there's so much bad advertising using an idea I picked up from a friend. It's cynical but it will explain things."

He took a pen and a piece of paper and drew a square in it.

"This square represents the universe of all the great ideas that can be used to solve a problem," he said. Then he drew a smaller square in that square.

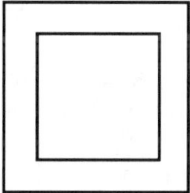

"This smaller square inside the first square represents the universe of great ideas you can come up with to solve a problem," he said. Then he drew a smaller square within that second square.

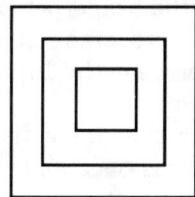

"This smaller square within the second square represents the universe of great creative ideas you can come up with that your creative director will buy," he said. Then, within this last square he drew a much smaller square "This tiny square represents the ideas that the client will pay for."

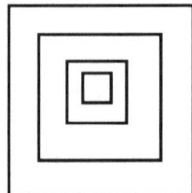

The moral of Terry's disquisition on advertising was clear. By the time you get through all the layers and filters and decision makers involved with making an advertisement, it's hard to come up with something good. There are too many people to satisfy, generally speaking. There are, of course, exceptions. Every once in a while you get a "good" client who gives the creative team lots of latitude. But that seems to be the exception rather than the rule.

## Mike Moser

At the time I spoke to him, Mike Moser was one of the principals of GMO. He resigned from the agency in July 1999 to spend more time with his family. I asked him how he worked. He broke advertising down into four components: the brand promise, the brand personality, the brand icon, and the brand values. He developed "roadmaps" for many of the products that GMO advertises such as Kia Motors America and Cisco Systems. We took Cisco Systems as a case study. He also is the person who thought up the line "Why 1984 won't be like '1984'" in the Apple ads, when he was part of Chiat/Day with Fred Goldberg and Brian O'Neill.

"The brand promise for Cisco Systems," he explained, "is that Cisco equals the Internet and that Cisco empowers people . . . we wanted to suggest that Cisco doesn't just connect computers . . . that is also connects people. For the brand personality, we wanted to give Cisco a positive image . . . to make it seem confident but not arrogant. We wanted to represent the Internet in a friendly way, to humanize it and Cisco Systems."

"You have to realize that advertising is selling, and when you're selling something, the message and the content of the message have to be considered, but also the personality of the salesman is important." "Next comes the brand icon. We made real people the symbol of Cisco . . . people who the people who saw the commercials could relate to. Cisco is an $8 billion company but we wanted it to have a human face. Last, comes brand values. We wanted to represent the Internet in a inspirational way, rather than using scare tactics."

I asked him about humor, because I had noticed that many of the GMO commercials on its reel were humorous.

"Humor's the easiest way to get in, to reach people emotionally. So we use charm and wit. Once we're in, that is, once we've got our target audience's attention and have established the brand, we can put in more content. Advertising is, in the final analysis, an art form. It's not a science."

I asked him to talk about one of his failures. He smiled . . . no doubt because it's always embarrassing to talk about one's failures. I told him about a friend of mine who is a package designer. He did a new package for an Italian salami company that had a lot of black in the label. It was a very handsome label but the black symbolized death to many people and the black heated the salami up so that it aged very quickly. Sales plummeted and the company quickly went back to a label with red, green, and white as the colors.

"We did a Rice-A-Roni advertisement that had prisoners, monks, and circus people in it," Moser said. "We were trying to be different so we could catch people's attention . . . but the people who saw the ads connected Rice-A-Roni with prison fare and with the meager meals monks eat . . . that kind of thing. We didn't understand the core values of the brand . . . and it didn't have the results we thought we'd get."

## Human Resources

I was scouting around for something to do after chatting with Mike Moser when I found Kimberly Gilbert from human resources who had a few free moments. I asked her how much stability there was in the industry and at GMO. "There's a fairly high turnover in our biggest departments—account management, media and traffic," she told me.

"I find that astonishing," I said.

"It's pretty much par for the course in all advertising agencies," she replied.

"So how do you find replacements?" I asked.

"We hire people from other agencies."

I immediately got a picture in my head of some kind of musical chairs in which account executives kept on moving from agency to agency . . . and I guess that image isn't too far from the truth. I asked her about how much advertising executives were paid. I was under the impression it was a high-paying profession.

"It's a low-paying industry, as a rule. But a really good copywriter, with 10 years experience, can make between $100,000 to $150,000 a year," she said. "GMO is lean and mean. So if we lose a big account, it isn't a disaster. We don't have to fire people. The personality profile for people in advertising is creative, aggressive, and energetic. Clients want things immediately."

I could see why all the energy was needed. Most of the people in the agency are young, and there are a very high percentage of women working here . . . and they work incredible hours . . . for relatively small salaries. I found that a real puzzle.

Kimberly gave me a Web site—jobstar.org—to go to that had salaries for many professions. I went to my cubicle and checked it out. I was astonished at the low starting salaries in the advertising business.

The next person I was to interview was a copywriter, who everyone calls "Q."

## Q (Real Name: Brian Quennell)

I had a chat with Q about copywriting and his work at GMO. I asked him about the way "creatives" use briefs. He is a tall, thin person who has an air of intensity about him.

"Some creatives don't follow briefs," he said, "and some creatives help write the briefs." And others, so I understand, fall in between these two poles of ignoring them and writing them.

"What advertising boils down to," he said, is "Hey, notice me" and "hey, like me!"

"Is it that simple," I asked.

He nodded his head.

He also used a word I often heard at GMO—*perceptions*. "You have to change people's perceptions," he said, "and then you've got to reinforce those changed perceptions."

I find the word *perception* interesting . . . because words and icons and visual images play such an important part in advertising. There are, of course, some commercials that hardly use any dialogue . . . or don't use any at all. They communicate by generating an attitude and use association and identification (of the viewer with the people in the commercial) to sell viewers.

I couldn't help but think about how complicated the matter really is and how difficult it is for advertising people to determine what impact advertisements actually have on people. That's why saying "run it up a flagpole and see if anyone salutes" makes sense.

You try something and see whether it works (having done research that suggests it might work). If it doesn't work, you try something else. But doing this, creating that 15 or 30 seconds worth of videotape, takes a mountain of work. An advertisement is a molehill on a mountain of labor

We then discussed how advertising helps shape people's consciousness.

"If you buy something because of the advertisement, then the advertisement becomes a benefit," he said. "That is, people often buy things because of the image that advertisement generates. The image, then, is part of the benefit of the product. People buy things because they expect to get some kind of a benefit . . . or a number of benefits. They'll look better, they'll feel better, they'll be able to do something they couldn't do before. So advertising becomes a vital part of the benefits that people expect to get out of the things they buy."

We talked a bit about the Cisco Systems account. "Eighty-five percent of the routers on the Internet are from Cisco Systems," he said. "Cisco is to the Internet what Intel is to computer chips and Microsoft to software. At first they thought they only needed to advertise it to the IT community, but then they realized they had to broaden their approach. So the agency came up with those television commercials. It was Jim Noble who came up with the idea for the kids. These commercials are very empowering and also edgy; they suggest you'd better get on the boat before it leaves. And the commercials were based on credible facts, too."

Q gave me a fascinating example of how the creative process works in advertising. An art director at GMO named Tito Melaga found a photo of a plane in the air that he really liked. This image then stimulated Q to write copy, based on the image. So it was a matter of chance and an image that created this print advertisement. It is always hard to figure out how something gets created and the ads Q wrote were based on serendipity. An image someone else liked generated an idea in Q and that led, eventually, to the ad. There's also Q's background and his history that played an important role.

"When I'm having a hard time thinking something up," he said, "I run through the seven deadly sins—sloth, envy, and so on—to look for ideas." What he was saying, I think, is that advertisers look for our primal urges, our basic instincts, to use in getting us to think what advertisers want us to think. As individuals we may not be influenced by a given print advertisement or radio or television commercial, but collectively—so I've argued in this book—we are profoundly affected by advertising socially and culturally.

## Lunch With Catrina?

I waited until 1 p.m. to go to lunch with Catrina, the woman who was more or less my sponsor at the agency. It was her decision to let me come in and snoop around. She is in constant motion and races from meeting to meeting. At 1 p.m. she suddenly appeared in my cubicle.

"I'm running late," she said. "And I've another meeting to go to." She chatted with me for a minute or two, and we decided to get together some other time—probably after my visit had ended.

I brought a sandwich with me to GMO assuming she wouldn't be able to make it. I thought it would be interesting to attach a meter to Catrina and see how many miles she logs in a given day, racing from meeting to meeting. She reminded me, in a curious way, of one of the characters in *Alice in Wonderland*—maybe it was the White Rabbit—who was always running around Wonderland saying "I'm late, I'm late."

## A Cynic Tells Me about One-Day Wonders

"We shouldn't give new people t-shirts and sweatshirts until the end of the day," one rather cynical person I met suggested, "because there have actually been a few one-day wonders. They come in, look around, and conclude they should leave. On the first day!"

That kind of behavior isn't typical, but the turnover of people at GMO, and all advertising agencies, seems considerable. Someone told me that the average stay for many people in an advertising agency is 2 or 3 years. So people in the advertising business, I can see, collect many sweatshirts and baseball caps. I got two very handsome sweatshirts and two baseball caps, and a Kia t-shirt.

"I made out like a bandit here," I told Fred, during one of our conversations. At that time I had only one sweatshirt. "The sweatshirt you left for me in my cubicle is extra large. It's enormous," I said.

Immediately Fred's executive assistant brought in a different kind of sweatshirt—handsome, black-zippered sweatshirt.

"Get him a red one," Fred said. I was wearing a red sweatshirt that had "Secret Agent" written on it, in white letters. It was a gift from my wife in 1970.

"There aren't any red ones left," she said.

"That black one is fine," I said. It was a large size and fit me much better than the first one I got. It didn't have the GMO logo on it, but on the back it read "good is the enemy of great." That's GMO's variation of the saying "best is the enemy of good." My wife thought it was very handsome when I brought it home.

## A Semiotic Analysis of the GMO Baseball Cap

I gave three workshops at GMO and in one of them, on applied semiotics, I analyzed the GMO baseball hat that has embroidered on the front "No shit." I discussed the baseball cap with its "No shit" on it. I knew what GMO thought it was communicating with this message—which is something like "we mean business," or "we don't horse around."

"But what does 'no shit' suggest, if we take it literally?" I asked. "Constipation!!

## A Chat with Fred Goldberg

I scheduled some time to chat with Fred Goldberg, and went to see him in his cubicle, just down the corridor from my cubicle. He has a corner cubicle—a signifier of power in the agency. And his cubicle is larger than those of many others, but he is, after all, the Chairman and CEO of the agency.

"Did you see this week's *20-20*?" he asked.

"No," I replied.

"Barbara Walters had a show about violence. They had videotapes of a bunch of little kids playing in a room full of toys. The little boys ignored most of the toys because they wanted to play with toy guns, which they found. They also found some ammunition and tried to load the ammunition in the guns. It was scary."

That led to a discussion of the amount of television people watch and its effects on them.

"The average person in America watches around 4 hours of television each day," I said. "The television set is on 7 hours, but different people are watching it during those 7 hours." He thought people watched more than 4 hours a day and called a colleague, who told him that I was correct. He asked me if I had any other questions about advertising or the agency, so we chatted for a while. We agreed to meet for lunch in a few weeks, after I had digested my experience at GMO, so I could tell him what I learned during my 3 weeks there. Then I had to race off to another appointment.

## John Nietzel

John started out at Leo Burnett in Chicago in its client service-training program. He worked in media for a couple of years and then got promoted into account management. I asked him about the Cisco Systems account because he had worked on it.

"Cisco Systems was spending less than $10 million on advertising a few years ago. The people running it realized they couldn't meet their goals at that level of expenditure, so in recent years, they've been spending a great deal more. Now they are spending around $60 million for advertising."

"We did a huge tracking study—Cisco Systems, you have to realize, has many businesses. There were 1,800 people in the study and we measured 23 different brand attributes. The results showed that the campaign is working. Sixty million dollars sounds like a lot of money, but you have to measure it against the $180 million that Lucent spent when it was launched."

"How many people does it take to service the Cisco Systems account?" I asked.

"Around 50, off and on," he said. "They don't work all the time on the Cisco Systems account. But it takes a lot of people."

I told him that I thought the Cisco Systems "Are You Ready?" commercials were quite handsome and very interesting.

"They've really had an impact," John said. "Don Listwin, one of the senior executives at Cisco Systems, presented the commercials to the sales force. He was so overcome by emotion when he showed them that he had to stop for a moment and pull himself together."

"We hired Stuart Douglas, one of the top directors in the world, for those commercials. He cost a small fortune . . . but he did a marvelous job of interpreting what Jim Noble, the creative director came up with . . . the idea of having all those kids and other people, from all over the place, talking about the Internet. The editing of those commercials also was very important."

"The people in planning found the facts that we used in the commercial. For example, we found out how many people join the Internet everyday. Then Q translated that information into something that people could grasp—namely, the fact that a group of people the size of England's population joins the Internet every day. He wrote the copy for the first three spots."

"I understand," I said, "that you've shot three more Cisco Systems commercials. Do you think they'll be as effective?"

"The second group won't be as shiny and new as the first three, but you've got to realize that 80% of the country hasn't seen the first three Cisco Systems commercials. They've only been used in spot markets so far. But the Cisco Systems campaign is going national."

I recalled a comment I made to Alan Kerr, a GMO vice president and group account director, who is involved with the Cisco Systems account. He had described the amount of money Cisco

Systems had been spending on advertising by moving his hand in a horizontal manner and then making a right angle and pushing his hand up toward the ceiling.

"Things are moving so fast we have to work really hard to keep up with them," he said.

"Alan . . . looks like you've got a tiger by the tail," I said.

He nodded. I'm not sure the expression on his face was that of worry or satisfaction, because I can imagine that Cisco will be doing more and more advertising, due to the success of the GMO campaign.

## Concluding Thoughts

This ethnology only gives a small portion of what I learned at GMO. I had never had my own cubicle before (if only for 3 weeks), and I found working in a cubicle a bit strange because I am used to the privacy of an office. I ate much too much ice cream (fortunately, for my cholesterol level, GMO lost the Dreyer's ice cream account and the ice cream was gone by the second week of my stay), and I ate too much pastry. I gave three workshops and GMO provided a big tray full of wonderful strawberries, cheesecakes, and other pastries for each workshop.

I found my stay at GMO fascinating. I met a number of people who told me a great deal about the advertising industry and about the campaigns for the products they worked on. I got a wonderful sense of what it is like working in an advertising agency . . . what problems people in advertising face and how difficult it is to create good advertisements.

I didn't use a taperecorder so my recreations of the dialogues are not always verbatim; I took notes when I chatted with people and in some cases wrote down what they said. I hope this essay-ethnography provides a sense of what working in an advertising agency is like. I don't think I discovered any secrets at GMO, but I do hope I have provided a picture of what advertising agencies are like. Most people haven't got the slightest idea of what goes on in advertising agencies and have very unrealistic ideas about them. Young men and women, reading this description of my stay at GMO, who see themselves as "drama queens or "drama kings," might even want to think about working in one.

I have one bit of advice for anyone who is thinking of going into advertising. If you do find a position in an advertising agency, *make sure it doesn't have an ice cream account!*

## THE AGENT IN THE AGENCY I: (1973) IN SEARCH OF THE QUINTESSENTIAL ENGLISHMAN

I spent a week at an advertising agency—one of the largest advertising agencies in the world, I believe, where I met various people in the place and got some kind of an idea about how English agencies work, and their particular image of the quintessential Englishman. It really was a wonderful opportunity to see an agency at work and talk with people in the advertising industry in an informal manner.

It all happened as a result of a letter that a friend wrote to a creative director at the agency. I telephoned Desmond S. (D.S.), walked in one day, said I would like to spend some time at the agency looking about and meeting people, and that was that! Quite remarkable. I used his office when he was out and about (that was frequent) and was passed around from person to person, so I could get the feel of the place and meet the personnel. It was all casual and unstructured, but I gained a good deal from it.

I had spent a bit of time at various U.S. agencies, talking to copywriters and creative directors, and I found that each agency has a particular character and flavor, a "style." In San Francisco, one agency reminded me of a prison—it was really slick and very chi-chi, but I felt trapped and found the place quite dehumanizing. People worked in little glassed-in boxes. around the perimeter of a large room; there was little privacy and it made me think of some kind of futuristic society in that people were at the beck and call of bells, buzzers, and the endlessly ringing telephone.

The person I spoke to at this agency was young and very hip—he had jeans on and was loose and casual, but I felt he was pushed in this direction to offset the oppressive ambiance of the office. The reception area was what might be called "futuristic-modern," with flashing lights indicating who was in, and all the standard futuristic flash—plastic, Danish teak, and so on.

The agency in London was much different . . . it was forced to be so by the nature of the buildings it occupied and, perhaps, by the tone of English business, that was quite low key and indirect, for the most part. At least at this level. It was certainly not postmodern, like many U.S agencies, at least the ones in New York that I visited a number of years before.

My host, D.S., did not look like the kind of person you would associate with an agency. He is a great big stout man, with a luxurious beard, thick glasses, who writes thrillers as an avocation. You don't get a sense of intensity from him—he seems to be very easy-going and casual, although I can't be sure that he really is like that. His office is messy and loose; it doesn't reflect pressure or concern with business in any way, although if you look at some of the notes that he scribbles to himself on large sheets of white paper you can see that there is a lot of thought beneath the facade of amiability.

He is the most senior "senior" creative director, and, as such, may be at a level relatively far removed from the day-to-day battles that go on in an agency and in the advertising world. There is, after all, competition and there are conflicting ideas within each agency as to the best way of proceeding in any given project. I had not seen him in action, so I had no real way of knowing what he is like at work, but I get "good vibrations."

He took me to meet another creative director, Tony P., with whom I had a long chat. I told him what I hoped to do and he had some interesting ideas and some good suggestions to make. I explained that I am interested in advertising because I believed that the people in the industry have a pretty good idea, based on experience and because that is what their job is about, of the essential aspects of English character. This must be broken down into the various class-level categories: A, B, C1, C2, D and E, and there are numerous other qualifications one must make, but nevertheless, the agencies know a hell of a lot about English taste, purchasing behavior, and by implication, values.

Tony said he thought that the English are a verbal rather than a visual society, a notion that I could accept, and told me about the remarkable longevity of certain English television programs and commercials. There is a strong sense of continuity in England, and the advertisements seem to take advantage of this. This has a number of advantages for the agency, in that it saves them "creative effort and energy." They can think up a campaign and perhaps get some kind of an appealing actor in it, and the rest is easy and just involves minor variations on the theme, so to speak. A campaign becomes a fugue with a dominant theme in numerous variations.

This kind of campaign also takes advantage of the power of iteration. People become used to a campaign, grow older with it, and it becomes part of them—acquiring meaning and significance (to them) over the years, the same way a comic strip becomes, in some strange way, part of their lives. Although similar things happen in America—in the Marlboro cigarette campaign—it is not as pronounced as in England. The royalists are loyalists, and the sense of history and tradition here supports the long-lived ad campaigns.

Tony suggested two important English artifacts that I should investigate: Bisto and other brown gravy mixes, and custard pudding mixes. These two items, he said, exercise an incredible role in the British diet, as I knew from experience.

I then visited a copywriter—a woman called "Sam"—who was working on a new cigarette campaign for a company interested in launching a king size. Because cigarettes are taxed on the weight of the tobacco in them, king-sized cigarettes are very expensive in England. They cost around 30p for 20 cigarettes, or U.S. 75 cents. The difficulty in writing ads for cigarettes is that you can't give them too strong a "personality," lest you *exclude* large numbers of people who won't like the cigarette's image, for one reason or another; but you still have to give people something tangible enough to attract them.

Sam was busy answering phones that were ringing one after the other; but we did manage to chat for 30 minutes or so. She told me that the mortality of cigarettes is great and that frequently it makes better sense to kill a brand and start a new one, than to pour money in to jazz up a fading one. It is the problem of good money after bad.

I could see that there was a dilemma in cigarette advertising. The copywriters are caught between the devil of exclusion of potential purchasers by too limited a personality or image and the deep blue sea of not gaining loyalty because of the cigarette's lack of definition and identity. There is also the matter of the hard sell and the fact that most people are aware, intellectually, that a cigarette is not much different from another one, despite the attempts of advertisers to suggest images and identities for their products.

Sam was in an office with a colleague who was on the phone a bit and then left. There were three phones in the office and she was never quite certain that one was ringing. It seems the English have not caught on to the phone with buttons that light up when a given extension is called.

After my talk with Sam I had lunch and then ended up chatting with two other creative directors, who were working on a presentation to be made to the government, for its campaign to cut down on the amount of electricity being used. The company had only 2 days to come up with a roughed up version of what it would do, and the person who was to make the presentation wasn't too certain about how good the concept was, but he was very cavalier about it all. After he left, I chatted with the other creative director, who was hanging around in case there was more work to be done on the campaign.

He gave me a short lecture on the way a creative director should work. His thesis was that it is imperative not to try too many different ways of solving a given problem (i.e., of developing a new theme for a given campaign) because this cost the agency a lot of money and tended to confuse the agency's customer, who really didn't know too much about what he wanted for his product. There should be, then, only one campaign suggested; it must be made to seem to be the only answer to the company's problems, so that the company's advertising director is sold before he or she sees the proposed advertisement.

In addition, the campaign must be kept for 6 or 8 years (or longer, if possible) so that the advertising agency doesn't have to go to the trouble of inventing a new campaign. It is easier to make variations on the given campaign than to think up new ones, and it costs a great deal less for the agency. It also may be in the best interest of the manufacturer, because the English tend to identify with long campaigns and the force of iteration is at work.

This was a valuable insight for me, because I could see that there is a kind of built-in resistance to change within a given agency. It costs them money to change a campaign, and there is the investment of the egos of the people in the agency, who worked on the product. Like all institutions, advertising agencies seek to maintain themselves, even maximize themselves, and expand, while their function then becomes secondary. This applies also to agencies, that are servants, but like many servants, are interested in serving themselves first—when they can arrange it. The agencies are businesses and their basic raison d'etre is to make a profit, as best they can. This is done by providing a service, but the agencies are essentially selfish; they want to provide as little service for as much profit as possible. They are, implicitly, conservative institutions although they make/affect great change in a given society.

At 3.30 p.m. I joined Tony and attended a meeting on a project that was being kicked around by the director of research, Pat R. He had in mind devising a new way of categorizing people—according to their visualizing proclivities as contrasted with the usual socioeconomic scale, the familiar A, B, C1, C2, D, and E. He had a Christmas card that he had bought at Woolworths and was trying to use it (and perhaps other similar artifacts) to get some kind of a reading on the way people see the world and themselves.

Ultimately, I imagined, this would link up with the socioeconomic scale, because there probably is a correlation between the visual sensibility of a person and his or her social class, but this remained to be seen. It was an attempt to do some "pure" research that has practical applications, but it was an extremely difficult subject that did not easily yield itself to research techniques. The people at the meeting decided it was worth pursuing even although nobody knew how to proceed.

## The Second Day

I spent my second day at the agency in random conversations, but that was rectified and some kind of a more structured program was arranged for me. Tony was going to take care of this.

My morning was spent talking with a member of some creative group who was unhappy because his wife of 9 years had just left him, taking their seven cats with her. A client had given him some expensive but rather sweet German wine, and we spent a few hours chatting about various things. One copywriter came in and announced that he had resigned.

I had heard about this the day before when I was walking around with D.S., and was surprised to see that he took it extremely casually, as if it were of no consequence whatsoever. When he was told about the resignation he said "Do you know why he did it?" "More money," was the answer. "Hmm sorry to lose him"; and with that the matter was dropped. Switching around from agency to agency is quite normal and is the best way to advance in the advertising world, so I have been told. This person was leaving a job as copywriter or member of a creative group and becoming a creative director, at a great increase in salary.

There is little or no resentment about people switching jobs and it isn't unusual for people who leave a company to return to it at a later date, although at a higher level. Thus the rapid turnover in agencies is structural—it is built into the industry and is forced upon people. I should imagine that this practice has some rather negative implications. Nobody is critically important, everyone is expendable; it all suggests that people in advertising are (as individuals) really of little consequence, and what is critical is the organization, not the capacities of people within it. Easy-go implies "who cares," and it strikes me that all of this is just the opposite of what might be imagined in advertising. Instead of finding individuality and uniqueness, and other phenomena like these that are associated with "creativity, we find a game of musical chairs in that creative people almost seem to be a dime a dozen, and in that there is little opportunity for writers and artists to do what they want.

These creative people seem to be terribly frustrated, because they must satisfy all kinds of people—their superiors, the companies purchasing advertising, and sometimes even publications that may reject a given advertisement. Sometimes they manage to salvage their ideas and identity and in rare cases are left alone (more or less), but even then, writing about soap and underarm deodorants is a bit of a bore after a while. Very few advertisements are lively and original and interesting and I should imagine the "romance" of it all withers after the fiftieth ad for lawn seed.

On the other hand, there is the intellectual problem of communicating to people, estimating their responses to a given presentation (advertisement) and considering alternative modes of presenting messages. Advertisers are practical individuals who have a mission—selling, both themselves and the products they are engaged to advertise—and who must have a grasp of their publics and audiences. It is fascinating at the theoretical level and tedious at the practical level, and because it attracts people who are frequently highly intelligent, articulate and sophisticated, it must be a trying job.

At noon, I went to the theater where a training film on package design was being shown. I wasn't able to watch all of it but did pick up on something that I find quite important. It showed a case history of a successful product in Britain—powdered milk, that is marketed here in 7-ounce tins (and also in larger tins, now). In the United States this product is marketed in three pound cartons or even larger plastic bags, that have enough milk to make twenty quarts of milk when it is reconstituted.

This product reflects two different worldviews, worldviews that are consequences of different levels of affluence, and different attitudes toward food, shopping, running a household, and a number of other related matters. The 7-ounce tin of powdered milk is an artifact to fit in another artifact we must consider—the shopping carts that housewives lug behind them, as they patrol the high roads and markets of Britain.

This milk is sold as an item to have on hand if one runs out of milk, but it suggests present-mindedness rather than future-mindedness, relative, that is, to the American sensibility. The English housewife purchases enough powdered milk to make three pints of milk: the American housewife purchases enough powdered milk to make 40 pints of milk, and at a much cheaper price per pint, also. This is made possible by the cheap packaging and large volume of the packages (and of the industry). Quite likely, American women use powdered milk differently from English women. It is not used as an emergency item but rather as a substitute for milk with a higher butterfat content (or a means of making 2% milk, which is very popular in America), and as a product that is considerably cheaper than whole milk.

### Third Day

My third day started off with a session at Pat R.'s office—he is the director of research for the agency. He brought in several of his colleagues and we spent the morning talking about some of their problems. One of his clients was pressing him to develop research techniques that might be especially appropriate to this client's products, but because there were only a limited number of techniques available, he had to invent jazzy names and mix up various techniques to satisfy this customer.

Advertising agencies face the same problems that all researchers in the social sciences face: there is a tendency to measure what is most easily measured, so that important phenomena, that are not susceptible to measurement are frequently overlooked. People have a great deal of confidence in numbers, but as the old saying goes, "figures don't lie, but liars figure." Very simple things such as recall and recognition can be measured easily, but these items may not be very important.

There has not been a great deal of work in applied aesthetics, and that, in fact, is what advertising research is really involved with. Advertising is a kind of applied art and we don't really know how to gauge the impact of art on people. Most advertising research, I would imagine, is similar in nature to most of the experimental work in psychology—it is focused around learning, for the simple reason that this is the area in which psychological research had made most of its advances, to this date.

The agency does have *probes,* in which a team of researchers go out into the field and ask housewives about their reasons for choosing various products. This is done in order to make sure that (to the degree this is possible) there is not a gap between the notions that creative directors have about people and the actual desires of people that is not too great. The idea is that actual contact with people helps give advertising people, and manufacturers of products, a more realistic conception of the public at large—or that section of the public that may be purchasing a given product.

I spent an hour talking about my work and the significance of McDonald's hamburgers and about color and desexualization in American culture. I hoped that I could make use of some of the findings of the advertisers for sociological reasons. We both wanted to know (i.e., I, as a scholar, and Pat as an advertising man) how people think and dream, what motivates them, what actuates them, what makes them reach out for one product or another, or one politician or another, or one philosophy or another. I was really dis-interested, in that I did not hope to affect people's behavior (except in a long range way, in terms of possible contributions to social policy), whereas Pat had very practical motives behind his activities.

He left with his colleagues for a marketing luncheon and I wandered off to see what was going on in the creative section of the agency. It turned out nothing was—it was the tag end of the year, so I spent the afternoon with my host or sponsor, D.S., talking about James Bond and pop culture. A group of people were gathered in his office, drinking whiskey and watching the dark evening envelop London. It was dark at four and there were few lights on in the office buildings around St. James Square.

I was invited to the agency office gala, so I spent the whole afternoon with D.S., and then we went to the hall where the party was being held. D.S. went ahead, but I hitched a ride in a long and elegant Rolls Royce that was ferrying some people there. Some people in the agency were beginning to worry about me. There was a rumor that I was a "time and motion" man, and when people asked me about this I always told them they would be declared redundant shortly. The agency did well in 1973, but economic conditions were so black and uncertain that a number of people were afraid they would be let go. Underneath the merriment of the party there lurked a gray melancholia that everyone seemed intent on blotting out by drinking.

I left the party quite early and wandered home via the underground, a bit high from drinking Scotch and a bit homesick, for D.S. had played lots of songs from the 1930s on his phonograph—Bing Crosby and others crooning tin pan alley stuff.

I had arranged with Tony to return in 2 weeks time, when the agency would be functioning normally and when I would be able to get a better grasp of the way people in advertising think. It was their perceptions of the English public that I was after, and although I didn't get what I was looking for in the 3 days I spent at the agency, I still learned a great deal. I was lucky in that people had time to talk with me about their work and about advertising. The secretaries had also given me a pretty good idea of the organizational structure of the agency and how it all worked—in theory at least.

Quite likely, I had all kinds of crazy ideas and erratic notions about the agency because I visited it at a most unusual time, but I did pick up vibrations and got to meet a number of people there (as a result of just wandering about) and I believe—or hope—that I did get a sense of the place, despite everything. There are some rather remarkable individuals there, brilliant people, whose efforts are "wasted" in rather trivial pursuits, in one sense, and perhaps monstrous ones, in another sense. Many of them have outside interests (D.S writes "cheap thrillers," as he put it) and seem to be in advertising because it pays well, is fascinating and allows them to pursue other interests.

My adventure at the agency was not yet complete; I was to return several times, for various things, and hoped that I would get a better reading on the place and get more of the kind of information I was looking for. D.S. and Tony (the two people with whom I spent most of my time with) had a lot of "juice" and were quite fabulous, although in entirely different ways, and I actually had a rather strong sense of kinship with them, although I may have been, in a certain sense, a snake in the garden. Maybe a worm would be a more suitable beast? I was not going to bite anyone and I was not looking for business secrets. All I wanted to do was to tap their brains, in a vague way, which is all that they want to do to everyone else, in a somewhat different way.

## THE AGENT IN THE AGENCY II: DAYS OF WHITES AND ROSES (AND A BIT OF COGNAC)

I returned to the advertising agency for a day following Tony around. I shadowed him—and was suitably dressed in my "Secret Agent" sweatshirt and track jacket. I arrived around 9:30 a.m. and he came in a short while later. We spent the early part of the morning chatting about advertising and such. He had to answer his phone because his secretary wasn't around for some reason. She called about 10:30 a.m. to say that she would be in; she had overslept.

The morning was devoted to a meeting about Martell Cognac. The agency had come up with a general theme and a slogan "Why don't we do this more often?" Tony was interested in making the phrase a bit more specific, and had written down a number of possibilities: "Martell me more often!" and "Why don't we Martell more often?" One of his art directors came in with some ads that were mock-ups of an idea he had—showing people reflected in a mirror—but it was somewhat hard to visualize what the real advertisement would look like. He also had some pictures of girls in front of blow-ups of the Martell label.

Two account executives were in the room and there was a considerable amount of discussion about the various suggestions. They had reactions to the proposals being made by the art director and Tony's suggested captions. They didn't think his proposed phrases were very interesting, and thought that it might be better to stick with the old general theme, but he argued that if they did they would lose readers. There was also a good deal of discussion about what Monsieur Martell, who was coming to London shortly, would like. They called him "the old man". Would "the old man" like this or that? Did he like paste ups that gave him options or did he like more or less finished campaign suggestions, although the latter might make him feel boxed in?

There was debate on how to get advertisements that were "interesting and provocative," and not just showcards. Tony said it was imperative that the campaign must be based on a question, "Why don't we?" being much better than "drink!" There was a good deal of talk about the kind of women to be used as models for the photos, and whether there need be a male figure in the photos.

It seems that their campaign was changing slightly. The "sentimentality and warmth" appeal was being dropped for a campy, sex and youth appeal, and they weren't trying to sell people on the idea of cognac but on their particular brand. They talked a great deal about the Smirnoff Vodka campaign that was a great success and that was based on sexploitation and the double entendre.

The problem they faced involved thinking up an advertisement that would command attention, that was original and that worked. There was some talk about thinking up some kind of a catchy phrase that would become part of the public currency, that comedians might repeat, and that might strike the public's fancy. After an hour or so of discussion the account executives left, and that problem (cognac) was left unresolved, although the art director promised to come up with some more work and Tony promised to do some more thinking about phrases.

I spent the afternoon listening in on another meeting, complete with media buyers, account executives, and creative people, that involved a German wine being sold by a big English distributor. The problem was how to utilize the English public's perceptions and notions about what "German-ness" (to coin a barbarism) is. The matter was further complicated by the fact that they were dealing with only a segment of the market, the lower end of the "up" market (that means middle class and above, trendy moderns in junior executive positions). Connoisseurs wouldn't be using the wine, except for Saturday lunches or something like that. So the top of the market was more or less written off: they were statistically negligible anyway.

A number of possible campaigns were proposed: one showing Germanic mood scenes, one showing elegant women in Germanic nightclubs, one showing blondes (girl of the month) and one a "calendar" ad. There were a few others, too: a comic Germanic script ad, and a gag ad showing a girl (nude with pubic hair) about to be raped, that was thrown in for comic relief.

The problem the group faced was finding a uniqueness and distinctiveness that would command a modicum of attention. In one issue of *Vogue* there were more than forty liquor ads and the problem of "clutter" is one that torments advertising executives. One ad, which showed a Germanic count leaning over a lovely lady, was scrapped, because it was "too much like Courvoisier." One ad that showed a lovely Schloss in an elegant mood scene was scrapped as not having enough impact; they also didn't know whether they could find enough interesting Germanic places to run a series.

They finally decided that their best and most promising possibilities were the blonde of the month and the calendar, both of that had the advantage (for the agency) of implying 12 advertisements, hence more money for the agency. When this subject was finished there was a discussion of yet another problem—a French sparkling white wine that was seeking identity and a place in the sun. The wine is more expensive than cheap sparkling wines but not as expensive as champagne. However, it could not be sold as a cheap substitute for champagne because there were other, cheaper substitutes. This wine was being sold as "the first new wine in 200 years." In fact, it was "invented" in the 1960s and had little pedigree.

Tony suggested that Bianca Jagger would be a good person with whom to associate the wine—as she was, at the time, one of the new aristocracy—perhaps what one might call the "celebritocracy"—the opinion leaders and style setters thrown up by the world of pop culture, who set trends and influence a vast number of "hip" people. There was a good deal of talk about not advertising the wine directly, but getting pop celebrities to use it and then keying in on this.

The account executive was eager to find a ritual with which to associate the wine. Champagne has certain associations in the public's mind: launching ships, weddings, festive occasions of a certain kind. What could this white wine "attach" itself to? "What about the loss of virginity?" suggested one wit. Someone else suggested the loss of male virginity, or an elegant breakfast of this wine and a few esoteric items.

The meeting was really an attempt to fashion an artificial mythology—to create another ritual that becomes, in time, taken for granted and natural to people. My day had been most curious: The morning was spent with Martell Cognac, then I saw a dozen Bisto ads and some Palmolive washing up ads, and then I returned to wines. I had been "down market" and "up market" and all over the place rather quickly.

One thing that I came away with was a realization that there is a great deal of intensive effort behind most advertisements—by people who are interested in locating their audience and appealing to it (or perhaps even manipulating it). This means that advertisements are repositories of cultural information; that they can be mined and can be "read" as expressions of a culture—as it is seen by a league of artists, writers and researchers. They work on the basis of their "image" of society and the sector of society they must appeal to, or are trying to appeal to. They may not be correct, but they cannot be ignored.

## THE AGENT IN THE AGENCY III: "WE ONLY GIVE PEOPLE WHAT THEY WANT!"

My friend Tony gave me a couple of speeches he had delivered in which he tried to explain advertising to people. One of his talks, "Are Consumerists Consumers?" makes the standard defense of advertising—We only give them what they want. He discusses what "they" like in another speech, "the importance of bad taste," in which he defines "bad taste" as

> anything that keeps a person "comfortable" in his situation and reactions, anything that soothes rather than stimulates, anything "dated" rather than "trendy", anything cozy in its values rather than spiky, anything cluttered rather than clean, anything familiar rather than unexpected, anything personal rather than educational in its values, anything sentimental rather than sophisticated, anything English rather than foreign, etc., etc.

This is the taste of more than 70% of the English public and it is this taste which, he argued, dictates to advertisers. He said:

> advertising does *not* lead. It only *follows*. It's a service of communication, or if you want it straighter, of *selling*, of a dialogue with consumers that is supposed to argue, cajole, or coax them into learning about goods for sale, depends (alas—because it would be *easier* that way) not on orders from manufacturers, or retailers, or providers of goods and services, but on *dictation* by the public. By a dictation from the public's instincts, or habits of mind or mindlessness, too strongly *entrenched* for mere word-spinners and picture-makers to do *anything* about.

Thus, concluded Tony, advertisers do not manipulate people. Just the opposite—they are "but putty in the public's soft and sweaty paw."

Now, all of this sounds very fine, and he may actually have believed it. The argument was persuasive, but it is not correct, for it makes a fundamental error—that the public's *instincts* are, somehow, sharply defined and not subject to "manipulation." It may be natural for one to drink and quench one's thirst, but it is not an instinct that leads one to do so with Coca-Cola, Pepsi-Cola, Stout, Beer, Chivas Regal, Schweppes, or what you swill. These wants are social. With few exceptions, people don't want anything unless they are taught (one way or the other) to want it by their culture. Advertisers are the unacknowledged legislators—perhaps even dictators—of taste in mankind.

What the public (or publics) wants is what it is told it should want; wants are created, not "givens" that are somehow discovered by corporations. Media, and in particular advertising, manufacture wants—often by creating anxiety in people or using the pressure of conformism or making use of the fact that many people imitate pop celebrities and other kinds of entertainment aristocrats.

This is all a matter of social-psychology. As Peter Berger (1963) said in *Invitation to Sociology: A Humanistic Perspective*:

> Society predefines for us that fundamental symbolic apparatus with which we grasp the world, order our experience and interpret our own existence. Society supplies our values, our logic and the store of information (or, for that matter misinformation) that constitutes our "knowledge." Very few people, and even they only in regard to fragments of this world view, are in a position to re-evaluate what has thus been imposed on them. They actually feel no need for reappraisal because the world view into which they have been socialized appears self-evident to them. Since it is also regarded by almost everyone they are likely to deal with in their own society, the world view is self-validating.

In other words, society legitimizes and organizes certain aspects of our lives for us, without our being aware of such things, frequently, and our illusion of perfect control over the contents of our minds makes us all the more susceptible to "direction."

Do English people buy *Bisto* gravy mix because it is natural and they have some kind of an instinctive need for it? Or, have they been taught to want it on the basis of a host of manufactured "feelings" that have cleverly been created around it, and that have been impressed upon their imaginations? Bisto is cornstarch and caramel that has been given charisma. It has become tied to all kinds of wholesome notions: heartiness, mother as provider of culinary treats, richness through deep color, family togetherness, love, and so on.

*Bisto* ads utilize certain vague notions in the public mind, such as the idea that dark gravy is good and rich. That notion may, in turn, have been manufactured earlier by other advertisers or may be part of folklore, or may even have some connection with ancient attitudes toward blood. Certainly a great deal of advertising makes use of the ideas people have about things, no matter how ridiculous they may be; but advertising also creates its own folklore and mythology, when it can.

There is a transformation process at work. Over time, that which was created and is artificial and un-natural takes on an aura of legitimacy, naturalness, normality, and becomes "traditional." When it reaches this stage, a product and its advertisement become part of folklore, and people do not recognize what has happened.

It is, of course, perfectly logical that new traditions arise, new folklore comes into being as the world turns and time ineluctably marches on. The problem: Who is creating this folklore (or fakelore) and for what purpose? Frequently the motives of people—and in particular the advertisers—who are so instrumental in creating this new folklore, are suspect. They wish to manipulate people and sell products, regardless of whether the products are good for people or not. The ordinary person's head is full of fantasy and myths, and these fantasies and myths have frequently been created by advertisers (either directly in ads or through programs sponsored, in America). Modern mythology is manufactured and commercial. The Marlboro cowboy, the "mum" serving Bisto, the "sucker" who needed Alka-Seltzer—all are manufactured heroes, and there are countless others.

Frequently, the public doesn't so much get what it wants as it gets a chance to select from what is available. There is a big difference. A person who buys a product at a market may do so for at least two reasons: First, he or she likes the product or second, there are no other products (alternatives) that the person might actually have preferred. Selection is not a guarantee of approval. This is why television rating services are so limited, despite their statistical proficiency. They can tell us what people are watching, but they can't tell us why people are watching a given program. They may be watching a program because "there's nothing better on."

Perhaps advertising doesn't so much give people what they want but rather convinces them to want what they get. There is a difference between getting what you want and wanting what you get. The latter involves a matter of selecting from what is available. Now it is quite possible that advertisers can convince people to like what they get—but it certainly isn't giving them what they want! In this respect, it can be argued that advertising has a very conservative aspect to it. It is not concerned with helping people acquire better taste but rather reinforces and strengthens (and plays on) "bad" taste. It is not concerned with developing human potentiality but rather with exploiting sexuality (and thereby devaluing it), with exciting people, with stirring them up, but only so it can channel this energy into consumption. It is, at best, amoral—and perhaps, all too frequently, immoral. Not so much because it lies to people, but because it uses them: it turns man's natural impulses against himself, so to speak.

## Chapter 9

# *Writing My Dissertation on* Li'l Abner

I was a student of literature and philosophy at the University of Massachusetts in Amherst, between 1950 and 1954. I wrote poetry and dabbled in occult religions (I was a reader, for a couple of years, at weekly seminars held by a Botany professor who was a theosophist. He had written a manuscript that I read from and that he then discussed.) I also worked at three jobs to help support myself, and read a lot of good literature. I graduated with a bachelor's degree in literature and a minor in philosophy. In addition, I took a number of art courses with the late Ian MacIver, who became a very good friend. Various professors in the English Department there told me I wouldn't be happy pursuing an advanced degree in literature because, as they put it, it tended to be highly technical and very specialized.

One of my favorite literature professors, Max Goldberg, said that really advanced companies made good use of English majors, and so I got an interview with one company—I think it was Vick's—that came to interview on campus. I chatted with the interviewer, who indicated that I wasn't the right person for Vick's. As I was leaving, he said to me, "Did you ever think of going into show business?"

I had decided to get a degree in journalism, since I liked to write, and went to the University of Iowa, in Iowa City, where I got a master's degree in magazine journalism. I also studied in the Writers Workshop there, with a really fantastic woman—Marguerite Young. She worked on a novel for 19 years. It was eventually published and remaindered several months after it was published. When I graduated in 1956, I was offered a job at *Better Homes & Gardens* in Des Moines, Iowa. The editor wanted to hire me but wasn't sure where I would fit in.

I was saved from life in Des Moines because I was drafted into the U.S. Army 11 days after I got my degree. In the army I was a feature articles writer in the Public Information Office of the Military District of Washington in Washington, DC. I also wrote high school sports for *The Washington Post* on weekend evenings, when I was free. After I was released from the army, I took the grand tour in Europe for a year and later worked in New York for a short period of time.

In 1960 I went to the University of Minnesota to work on a doctoral degree in American studies. When I described the program at Minnesota to my brother, who is an artist, he told me "American studies is a Shmoo. If you roast it, you're a literature scholar. If you fry it, you're a historian. If you boil it, you're a sociologist. If you bake it, you're a political theorist. Better to profound yourself in a discipline." The Shmoo was a character in Al Capp's famous comic strip *Li'l Abner*. As Capp described this mythical little beast in his strip,

> Fry a Shmoo and it comes out chicken. Broil it and it comes out steak. Shmoo eyes make splendid suspender buttons. Shmoo hide cut thin is fine leather; cut thick, it is the best lumber. Shmoo whiskers make magnificent toothpicks.

I liked American studies because it allowed me to design a program of study to suit my interests and I thought a multidisciplinary approach made a great deal of sense, especially when it came to understanding American culture and society. So I took courses on subjects such as American intellectual history with David Noble, political theory with Mulford Q. Sibley, social thought with Ralph Ross, and American literature with a variety of professors. I also taught a couple of courses for the English Department and was a teaching assistant for a philosophy professor, May Brodbeck and for an English professor, Brom Weber, who taught a course on American humor.

One course I took turned out to be very important for my career. I took a course on American political thought with Mulford Q. Sibley, a professor of political science, that was to lead to my choice of a dissertation topic. He posted a list of possible term paper topics on his door and I decided to write on political aspects of Al Capp's comic strip, *Li'l Abner*. I chose this topic because I was interested in humor and also because I am a cartoonist and illustrator, so I have always been interested in comics.

By chance, I had met Al Capp at a party his daughter had in Cambridge a number of years earlier. His daughter was studying art with my brother at the Museum of Fine Arts art school in Boston, and she told him about a party she was having and he told me about it. I didn't know it was to be at the home of Al Capp who drew *Li'l Abner* when I went to the party and remember spending a good deal of time chatting with him that night.

Several years after taking that course in American political thought, I made an appointment to talk with Sibley about my dissertation subject. I thought I might write on utopian thought, which interested me a great deal and which seemed to be a suitably serious subject that the American studies council, which evaluated dissertation proposals, would accept. It was made up of professors drawn from the humanities and social sciences.

I walked in to see Sibley with the notion of writing about utopian thought and walked out with *Li'l Abner*. "You've already written on *Li'l Abner*," he said. "Why not expand that essay you wrote for my American political thought course into your dissertation? You're interested in humor and you're an artist," he continued. "Take my advice and write on *Li'l Abner*." And so, I walked out of his office with a new dissertation subject, *Li'l Abner*.

I submitted a proposal in which I said I wanted to analyze *Li'l Abner* and relate it to American culture, and, as I understand it, the professors from the humanities were outraged—that I would do a dissertation on something as trivial as a comic strip. They wanted to reject the subject of my proposal, but the social scientists supported my proposal, so I was told to rewrite my proposal on *Li'l Abner* and resubmit it.

I went to a literature professor, who was the head of the American studies council, and he suggested that I be more specific in my proposal and say that I would analyze *Li'l Abner* in terms of its language, its narrative structure, its graphic aspects, and its satirical tone. So I revised my proposal and passed it in. To my great relief, it was accepted and so I ended up writing my dissertation on a comic strip, *Li'l Abner*. It was, I believe, the first dissertation written on a comic strip in an American university.

Most of the PhD graduate students in American studies laughed when they heard what I was going to write my dissertation on. They all had "serious" and "important" subjects and considered my writing on a mere comic strip, something they used to wrap garbage with, quite absurd.

In 1963, I won a Fulbright to Italy and ended up in Milan to do some research on the Italian magazine press. I actually did research on these publications and my article on these magazines was published in an Italian social science journal, *Il Mulino*. I taught two courses in American studies at the University of Milan. One day, I asked my students who was doing interesting work in Italy and they all gave me the same name—Umberto Eco. He taught at the University of Bologna but lived in Milan, so I called him and got to know him. We met at the Galleria in Milan and I was to see him, and some of his colleagues who were interested in popular culture, off and on, during the year.

He was, it turns out, very much interested in popular culture and, in particular, in comics. I got to know a number of people doing work on comics in Italy and went to various publishers who were putting out collections of comics. I also started studying Italian comics. My boss at the University of Milan, Agostino Lombardo, had a journal, *Studi Americani*, and he asked me to write an article for him on Italian and American comics. So I made a comparative study of American and Italian comics that were similar in terms of when they appeared and subject matter and published in it his journal. I included some of this material in the first chapter of my dissertation, which dealt with popular culture and the comics and was a defense of the value of studying popular culture, in general, and comics, in particular.

I was greatly encouraged by the work the Italians were doing in popular culture and in comics and felt it validated my work. When I returned from Italy, I finished my dissertation and graduated from the University of Minnesota in 1965. I can remember the graduation. Someone, perhaps the president of the university, announced the name of the person getting his or her doctorate and the subjects of this person's dissertation. After each name and dissertation subject was announced, the audience applauded. When my subject was announced, "*Li'l Abner*: An American Satire," people in the audience laughed.

And so the very first thing that happened after I earned my doctorate and entered academic life was that people laughed at my choice of a dissertation topic. But I was to have the last laugh, for my dissertation was accepted for publication and appeared in 1970 as *Li'l Abner: A Study in American Satire*. It was also republished a number of years later in a series the University of Mississippi Press put out on classic works in popular culture. In 1970, an article I wrote about attitudes on authority appeared in a distinguished social science journal, *Transaction* (now renamed *Society*) and I was to eventually have a long relationship with the editor of this journal, Irving Louis Horowitz, and publish a number of books on humor, media and popular culture with Transaction Publications.

My interest in comics led to work on other forms of popular culture and to the mass media, as well. I wrote on advertising, professional wrestling, television shows, fast foods, humor, fashion, and numerous other aspects of popular culture and everyday life. I once wrote an article that asked "Why is popular culture unpopular?" My answer was that it was popular with the masses—and unpopular with certain elites who looked down on ordinary people and their tastes. Investigating this subject has, it turned out, been the work of my life and I have spent almost 40 years studying the media, popular culture, and everyday life, trying to figure out why people feel the way they do about it and what impact it may be having on our lives and our societies.

One wonderful thing about popular culture is that new developments keep happening all the time. Just when you think you've seen everything, something new comes along that blows your mind. And so you've got to get to work and see if you can figure out what is going on.

I should add that popular culture and the media are now considered valid and important subjects, and scholars from many different disciplines are now investigating these subjects. All of a sudden, people realized that popular culture is a kind of culture and culture has now become an important subject in the academy. What used to be called popular culture has transmogrified into a "hot" discipline called cultural studies, and now everyone (i.e., scholars from many disciplines) is getting into the act. Books on various aspects—one might say all conceivable aspects—of cultural studies are being published in incredible numbers.

In recent years, I have adapted the murder mystery and used it to write satirical mysteries that ridicule academics and university types and also function as textbooks. My first comic mystery was *Postmortem for a Postmodernist*. A reviewer said he wasn't sure whether it was a textbook pretending to be a mystery or a mystery pretending to be a textbook, but in any case, it was suitably postmodernist. And now I have another comic mystery that deals with mass communication theorists who kill one another off, titled *The Mass Comm Murders*, in press.

So, it seems that I'm having the last laugh . . . and if I'm not amusing anyone else, at least I'm amusing myself. That is, I believe, one of main the benefits of becoming a senior citizen.

# Chapter 10

## *Conclusions*
## *Survivors of* Survivor
## *and Other Pop Culture Crazes*

There is no satisfactory conclusion to a book on popular culture. Just when you think you have seen everything, something new comes along . . . and the country becomes transfixed by programs like *Who Wants to be a Millionaire* and *Survivor* (and soon, a host of other so-called "reality" television shows). That is because television and other media are desperate for content and when they find something that strikes some kind of a responsive chord, they jump on the bandwagon, hoping they will be in time, to use surfer lingo, to "catch the wave."

What I have done in this book is to alert readers to the role popular culture plays in our lives and to suggest a number of ways to analyze and interpret popular culture. That is, I have asked my readers to look at popular culture and the media in terms of how they achieve their effects and how they may be influencing us—often without our recognizing what is happening to us. Since I have suggested that we are all (I hope) Survivors of the hit television program *Survivor,* let me say something about the show.

### Survivor

When you have a megahit popular culture phenomenon like *Survivor,* the immediate questions you have to ask yourself are:

1. What is the significance of the reality genre?
2. Why was this show so popular?
3. What, if anything, does it reflect about American culture and society?

The show is one example of a number of programs that are classified as so-called "reality" shows—shows that use real people, not actors, who interact with one another in various ways. The people are put into some kind of an unusual and highly contrived situation and the show is based on their actions and their relations with others. There is usually some prize given to whomever "wins" the game.

The people who were in *Survivor* talked about it as a game that they were playing and as such, they formed alliances, double-crossed one another, did whatever they could to win. I would like to suggest that one of the reasons *Survivor* was so popular was that it was a combination of a number of different genres. Let me list them and explain.

> **A soap opera:** The show was full of intrigues and conversations among various players about what they were going to do when they had their tribal council and had to kick someone off the island. There wasn't any romance involved but the relationships, full of gossip and scheming, were very similar in nature to what one finds in soap operas.
>
> **A nature show:** The people in *Survivor* were on an island that they shared with all kinds of animals. The sense of place of the show gave it an aura of a nature show.
>
> **A game show:** In every episode there was an "immunity challenge" in which members were asked to compete in some strange activity. Whoever won the "immunity challenge" was given a necklace symbolizing immunity, which meant they couldn't be kicked off the island. This element in the show reminded me of summer camps where there are organized competitions.
>
> **A beach-bunny show:** Because the people in *Survivor* were on an island with sandy beaches, the women often wore skimpy bikinis, so there was a lot of flesh showing in the program.
>
> **A documentary:** Because the show was about real people, it had an element of the documentary about it. Documentaries are often described as creative interpretations of reality and *Survivor* would fit under that definition. There were elements of *Survivor* that suggested the program was about a group (tribe?) of

people who were forming primitive institutions and were involved in strange rituals, although these contrived rituals—such as the tribal council—were imposed on them by the creators of the show. It was a documentary about a pseudo-tribe of people living in a jungle island. Documentaries often shoot 50 or 100 hours, which they reduce greatly—often to less than 1 hour.

That is an important matter for although the show featured real people and not actors and actresses, it was highly edited. It wasn't reality, per se, but the reality *Survivor's* editors imposed on the program. It was this use of editing that enabled the program's director to generate excitement and drama in the production. There was a lot of quick-cutting, there were many vignettes, there was some talking directly into the camera by the players—all of which are editing tricks used by the director of the show. They did a beautiful job, because *Survivor* was an exciting and very dramatic show.

The show used real people and not actors, but it would be fair to say that the show was "cast" by the production team responsible for the show. The show was successful, in part, because the director was able to find a group of interesting people, with whom members of the audience could connect. It might be suggested that one of the reasons for the success of *Survivor* was the members of the audience were searching for connections with others and *Survivor* provided the audience with a false sense of intimacy with the people on the island. Technically, this is known as a para-social relationship, a feeling people who watch serial television programs have that they really "know" the characters they are watching.

As I watched *Survivor,* I could not help but think about another popular show that was just the opposite of *Survivor*—namely *The Prisoner*. The hero of this show, a spy who has resigned, spends 17 episodes trying to get off an island to which he has been mysteriously transported. In *Survivor,* everyone was trying to stay on the island as long as possible, in order to win $1 million.

## Sociocultural Significance of *Survivor*

*Survivor* has been the subject of numerous articles by culture critics and media scholars, who dealt with its cultural and social significance. Some said it was popular because people identified with its dog-eat-dog qualities, and saw Rich, the winner of the first show's game, as a charming schemer, who figured out what he had to do to win and acted on his plans. Others have said just the opposite, that it reflected the importance of cooperation among members of society and that Rich won because the person he made his alliance with stuck to his word.

I argue that there were a number of factors that contributed to the show's success and that it was such a complex text that one can read all kinds of different things into it. But we must remember that it was a show that was contrived, whose origins were elsewhere (it was one of a number of reality shows that got started in Europe), and that, as reader-response critics keep telling us, different people see different things in the show. One thing the show teaches us is that there are many people whose personalities are interesting to us and who can, thanks to the magic of editing, "act." Many of the members of the program are doing commercials now and have other opportunities. Being in the public's eye for a number of weeks has, it seems, economic value. So even those who didn't survive to the very end seem to be winning something.

The term *survivor* is interesting. It comes from the Latin *supervivere—super* means "over" and *vivere* means "to live." *Survivor* means to live longer, to persist, to outlast others. There is something a bit negative about the term, as I see things. There is, for example, a difference between surviving and triumphing. Surviving suggests you just made it; triumphing suggests you have a glorious win. Does the popularity of *Survivor* suggest Americans see themselves as a nation of people who have to do whatever they can just to survive? This hardly seems likely in the economic book times of 2000 AD, but it may be that a large number of people do worry about surviving—especially young people who, statistics tell us, were drawn to the show in large numbers—much to the delight and profit of CBS.

As I wrote this, CBS was preparing a new *Survivor* show, to take place in Australia and was worrying why another of its reality shows wasn't doing well. So much in the media, in the arts, and in life is chance. It was interesting to see that the new *Survivor* caught the attention of the American public the way the first show did.

I hope that readers of this book will have learned how to analyze it and any other television show, film, or, generally speaking, example of popular culture that interests them. If that happens, and my readers learn how to adopt an analytic view of the mass media, popular culture, and everyday life, my fondest hopes for this book will have been realized. For then, my readers will have become more than survivors of *Survivor*.

# References

Abrams, M.H. (1958). *The Mirror and the Lamp.* New York: Norton.

Berger, Arthur Asa. (1998). *Media Analysis Techniques* (2nd ed.). Thousand Oaks, CA: Sage.

Berger, Peter. (1963). *Invitation to Sociology.* Garden City, NY: Anchor.

Bloom, Allan. (1983, May 2). Cited in "Notable and Quotable." *Wall Street Journal.*

Borges, Jorge Luis. (1964). *Other Inquisitions: 1937-1952.* Austin: University of Texas Press.

de Certeau, Michel. (1984). *The Practice of Everyday Life* (S. Rendall, Trans.). Berkeley: University of California Press.

Featherstone, Mike. (1991). *Consumer Culture & Postmodernism.* London: Sage.

Gans, Herbert. (1974). *Popular Culture and High Culture.* New York: Basic Books.

Girard, René. (1991). *A Theatre of Envy.* Oxford: Oxford University Press.

Huizinga, J. (1924). *Waning of the Middle Ages.* New York: Doubleday Anchor.

Iyer, Pico. (1993). *Falling off the Map.* New York: Knopf.

Lakoff, G., & Johnson, M. (1980). *Metaphors We Live By.* Chicago: University of Chicago Press.

Leach, Edmund. (1970). *Claude Lévi-Strauss*. New York: Viking Press.

LeBon, G. (1960). *The Crowd: A Study of the Popular Mind*. New York: Viking.

Lull, James. (1992). *Popular Music and Communication*. Thousand Oaks, CA: Sage.

Lyotard, Jean-François. (1984). *The Postmodern Condition: A Report on Knowledge*. Minneapolis: University of Minnesota Press.

Mannheim, K. (1936). *Ideology and Utopia* (L. Wirth & E. Shils, Trans.). New York: Harcourt, Brace.

Real, Michael R. (1989). *Supermedia: A Cultural Studies Approach*. Newbury Park, CA: Sage.

Rios, Al, & Jack Stout. (2000). *Positioning: The Battle for Your Mind*. New York: McGraw-Hill.

Saussure, Ferdinand de. (1966). *Course in General Linguistics* (W. Baskin, Trans.). New York: McGraw-Hill.

# Suggested Readings

Adorno, Theodor W. (1967). *Prisms* (S. Weber & S. Weber, Trans.). Cambridge: MIT Press.

Adorno, Theodor W. (1991). *The Culture Industry: Selected Essays on Mass Culture.* London: Routledge.

Aronowitz, Stanley. (1992). *The Politics of Identity.* New York: Routledge.

Aronowitz, Stanley. (1993). *Dead Artists, Live Theories and Other Cultural Problems.* New York: Routledge.

Armstrong, Nancy. (1987). *Desire and Domestic Fiction: A Political History of the Novel.* New York: Oxford University Press.

Bakhtin, M.M. (1981). *The Dialogic Imagination* (C. Emerson & M. Holmquist, Trans., M. Holmquist, Ed.). Austin: University of Texas Press.

Bakhtin, Mikhail. (1984). *Rabelais and His World* (H. Iswolsky, Trans.). Bloomington: Indiana University Press

Bal, Mieke. (1985). *Narratology: Introduction to the Theory of Narrative.* Toronto: University of Toronto Press.

Barker, Martin & Ann Beezer. (1992). *Reading into Cultural Studies.* London: Routledge.

Barthes, Roland. (1970). *Writing Degree Zero & Elements of Semiology* (A. Lavers & C. Smith, Trans.). Boston: Beacon Press.

Barthes, Roland. (1972). *Mythologies* (A. Lavers, Trans.). New York: Hill & Wang.
Barthes, Roland. (1977). *Empire of Signs* (S. Heath, Trans.). New York: Hill & Wang.
Barthes, Roland. (1988). *The Semiotic Challenge* (R. Howard, Trans.). New York: Hill & Wang.
Bateson, Gregory. (1972). *Steps to an Ecology of Mind*. New York: Ballantine Books.
Baudrillard, Jean. (1983). *Simulations* (P. Foss, Trans.). New York: Semiotext(e).
Baudrillard, Jean. (1996). *The System of Objects* (J. Benedict, Trans.). London: Verso.
Beilharz, Peter, Gillian Robinson, & John Rundell. (1992). *Between Totalitarianism and Postmodernity: A Thesis Eleven Reader*. Cambridge, MA: MIT Press.
Bennett, Tony & Janet Woollacott. (1987). *Bond and Beyond: The Political Career of a Popular Hero*. New York: Methuen.
Berger, Arthur Asa. (1973). *The Comic-Stripped American*. New York: Walker.
Berger, Arthur Asa. (1975). *The TV-Guided American*. New York: Walker.
Berger, Arthur Asa. (1984). *Signs in Contemporary Culture: An Introduction to Semiotics*. New York: Annenberg-Longman.
Berger, Arthur Asa. (1989). *Seeing is Believing: An Introduction to Visual Communication*. Mountain View, CA: Mayfield.
Berger, Arthur Asa. (1990). *Agitpop: Political Culture and Communication Theory*. New Brunswick, NJ: Transaction Books.
Berger, Arthur Asa. (1993). *An Anatomy of Humor*. New Brunswick, NJ: Transaction Books.
Berger, Arthur Asa. (1994). *Blind Men and Elephants: Perspectives on Humor*. New Brunswick, NJ: Transaction Books.
Berger, Arthur Asa. (1994). *Cultural Criticism: A Primer of Key Concepts*. Thousand Oaks, CA: Sage.
Berger, Arthur Asa. (1997). *Postmortem for a Postmodernist*. Walnut Creek, CA: AltaMira Press.
Berger, Arthur Asa. (2000). *Ads, Fads and Consumer Culture*. Boulder, CO: Rowman & Littlefield.
Berger, Arthur Asa. (2001). *Jewish Jesters*. Cresskill, NJ: Hampton Press.
Berman, Marshall. (1982). *All That is Solid Melts Into Air: The Experience of Modernity*. New York: Touchstone Books.
Bernstein, Richard J. (1992). *The New Constellation: The Ethical-Political Horizons of Modernity/Postmodernity*. Cambridge, MA: MIT Press.

Best, Steven & Douglas Kellner. (1991). *Postmodern Theory*. New York: Guilford.
Bettelheim, Bruno. (1976). *The Uses of Enchantment*. New York: Knopf.
Blau, Herbert. (1992). *To All Appearances: Ideology and Performance*. London: Routledge.
Bogart, Leo. (1985). *Polls and the Awareness of Public Opinion*. New Brunswick, NJ: Transaction Books.
Bolter, Jay David & Richard Grusin. *Remediation: Understanding New Media*. Cambridge, MA: MIT Press.
Bowlby, Rachel. (1993). *Shopping with Freud: Items on Consumerism, Feminism and Psychoanalysis*. London: Routledge.
Brenkman, J. (1993). *Straight Male Modern: A Cultural Critique of Psychoanalysis*. New York: Routledge.
Brenner, Charles. (1974). *An Elementary Textbook of Psychoanalysis*. Garden City: Anchor Books.
Brown, Mary Ellen. (Ed.). (1990). *Television and Women's Culture: The Politics of the Popular*. Newbury Park, CA: Sage.
Brown, Mary Ellen. (1994). *Soap Opera and Woman's Talk: The Pleasure of Resistance*. Thousand Oaks, CA: Sage.
Buck-Morss, Susan. (1989). *The Dialectics of Seeing: Walter Benjamin and the Arcades Project*. Minneapolis: University of Minnesota Press.
Butler, Judith. (1993). *Bodies That Matter*. New York: Routledge.
Cantor, Muriel G. (1988). *The Hollywood TV Producer*. New Brunswick, NJ: Transaction Books.
Cantor, Muriel G. & Joel M. Cantor. (1991). *Prime-Time Television: Content and Control*. Thousand Oaks, CA: Sage.
Carey, James. (Ed.). *Media, Myths and Narratives: Television and the Press*. Newbury Park, CA: Sage.
Clarke, John. (1992). *New Times and Old Enemies: Essays on Cultural Studies and America*. London: Routledge.
Collins, Richard, James Curran, Nicholas Garnham, & Paddy Scannell. (Eds.). (1986). *Media, Culture & Society: A Critical Reader*. Newbury Park, CA: Sage.
Coward, Rosalind & John Ellis. (1977). *Language and Materialism: Developments in Semiology and the Theory of the Subject*. London: Routledge & Kegan Paul.
Crane, Diane. (1992). *The Production of Culture: Media and the Urban Arts*. Newbury Park, CA: Sage.
Creed, Barbara. (1993). *The Monstrous-Feminine: Film, Feminism, Psychoanalysis*. London: Routledge.
Creedon, Pamela J. (1993). *Women in Mass Communication* (2nd Ed.). Thousand Oaks, CA: Sage.

Crook, Stephen, Jan Pakulski, & Malcolm Waters. (Eds.). (1992). *Postmodernization: Change in Advanced Society*. London: Sage.
Cross, Gary. (1993). *Time and Money: The Making of a Consumer Culture*. London: Routledge.
Culler, Jonathan. (1975). *Structuralist Poetics: Structuralism, Linguistics and the Study of Literature*. Ithaca, NY: Cornell University Press.
Culler, Jonathan. (1977). *Ferdinand de Saussure*. New York: Penguin Books.
Culler, Jonathan. (1981). *The Pursuit of Signs*. Ithaca, NY: Cornell University Press.
Culler, Jonathan. (1982). *On Deconstruction*. Ithaca, NY: Cornell University Press.
Danesi, Marcel. (1994). *Messages and Meanings: An Introduction to Semiotics*. Toronto: Canadian Scholars Press.
Danesi, Marcel & Donato Santeramo. (Eds.). (1992). *Introducing Semiotics: An Anthology of Readings*. Toronto: Canadian Scholars Press.
Davis, Robert Con & Ronald Schleifer. (1991). *Criticism & Culture*. London: Longman.
de Certeau, Michel. (1986). *Heterologies: Discourse on the Other* (B. Massumi, Trans.). Minneapolis: University of Minnesota Press
Denney, Reuel. (1989). *The Astonished Muse*. New Brunswick, NJ: Transaction Books.
Denzin, Norman K. (1991). *Images of Postmodern Society: Social Theory and Contemporary Cinema*. London: Sage.
Doane, Mary Ann. (1991). *Femmes Fatales*. New York: Routledge.
Donald, James & Stuart Hall (Eds.). (1985). *Politics and Ideology*. Bristol, PA: Taylor & Francis.
Douglas, Mary. (1975). *Implicit Meanings: Essays in Anthropology*. London: Routledge & Kegan Paul.
Douglas, Mary. (1992). *Risk and Blame: Essays in Cultural Theory*. London: Routledge.
Duncan, Hugh Dalziel. (1985). *Communication and the Social Order*. New Brunswick, NJ: Transaction Books.
Dundes, Alan. (1987). *Cracking Jokes: Studies in Sick Humor Cycles and Stereotypes*. Berkeley, CA: Ten Speed Press.
Durkheim, Emile. (1967). *The Elementary Forms of the Religious Life*. New York: The Free Press.
Dyer, Richard. (1993). *The Matter of Images: Essays on Representations*. London: Routledge.
Eagleton, Terry. (1976). *Marxism and Literary Criticism*. Berkeley: University of California Press.

Eagleton, Terry. (1983). *Literary Theory: An Introduction.* Minneapolis: University of Minnesota Press.

Easthope, Antony. (1991). *Literary into Cultural Studies.* London: Routledge.

Eco, Umberto. (1984). *The Role of the Reader.* Bloomington: Indiana University Press.

Elam, Keir. (1980). *The Semiotics of Theatre and Drama.* London: Methuen.

Ettema, James S. & D. Charles Whitney (Eds.). (1994). *Audiencemaking: How the Media Create the Audience.* Thousand Oaks, CA: Sage.

Ewen, Stuart. (1976). *Captains of Consciousness.* New York: McGraw-Hill.

Ewen, Stuart & Elizabeth Ewen. *Channels of Desire: Mass Images and the Shaping of American Consciousness.* New York: McGraw-Hill.

Fiske, John & John Hartley. (1978). *Reading Television.* London: Methuen.

Fiske, John. (1989). *Reading the Popular.* London: Routledge.

Fiske, John. (1989). *Understanding Popular Culture.* London: Routledge.

Featherstone, Mike. (Ed.). (1988). Postmodernism. *Theory, Culture & Society,* 5(2-3).

Fjellman, Stephen M. (1992). *Vinyl Leaves: Walt Disney World and America.* Boulder, CO: Westview.

Franklin, Sarah, Celia Lury, & Jackie Stacey. (1992). *Off-Centre: Feminism and Cultural Studies.* London: Routledge.

Freud, Sigmund. (1960). *A General Introduction to Psychoanalysis* (J. Riviere, Trans.). New York: Washington Square Press.

Freud, Sigmund. (1963). *Jokes and Their Relation to the Unconscious* (J. Strachey, Trans.). New York: W.W. Norton.

Freud, Sigmund. (1965). *The Interpretation of Dreams* (J. Strachey, Trans.). New York: Avon.

Frith, Simon. (1981). *Sound Effects: Youth, Leisure and the Politics of Rock and Roll.* New York: Pantheon.

Fry, William F. (1968). *Sweet Madness: A Study of Humor.* Palo Alto, CA: Pacific Books.

Gandelman, Claude. (1991). *Reading Pictures, Viewing Texts.* Bloomington: Indiana University Press.

Garber, Marjorie. (1993). *Vested Interests: Cross-Dressing and Cultural Anxiety.* New York: HarperPerennial.

Garber, Marjorie, Jann Matlock, & Rebecca Walkowtiz. (Eds.). (1993). *Media Spectacles.* New York: Routledge.

Garber, Marjorie, Pratibha Parmar, & John Greyson. (Eds.). (1993). *Queer Looks: Perspectives on Lesbian and Gay Film and Video.* New York: Routledge.

Gitlin, Todd. (1985). *Inside Prime Time.* New York: Pantheon.

Goldstein, Ann, Mary Jane Jacob, Anne Rorimer, & Howard Singerman. (1989). *A Forest of Signs: Art in the Crisis of Representation.* Cambridge, MA: MIT Press.

Greenblatt, Stephen J. (1992). *Learning to Curse: Essays in Early Modern Culture.* New York: Routledge.

Grossberg, Lawrence. (1992). *We Gotta Get Out of This Place: Popular Conservatism and Postmodern Culture.* New York: Routledge.

Grossberg, Lawrence, Cary Nelson, & Paula Treicher. (1991). *Cultural Studies.* New York: Routledge.

Grotjahn, Martin. (1966). *Beyond Laughter: Humor and the Subconscious.* New York: McGraw-Hill.

Guiraud, Pierre. (1975). *Semiology.* London: Routledge & Kegan Paul.

Gumbrecht, Hans Ulrich. (1992). *Making Sense in Life and Literature* (G. Burns, Trans.). Minneapolis: University of Minnesota Press.

Habermas, Jurgen. (1987). *The Philosophical Discourse of Modernity: Twelve Lectures* (F.G. Lawrence, Trans.). Minneapolis: University of Minnesota Press.

Habermas, Jurgen. (1989). *The New Conservatism: Cultural Criticism and the Historians' Debate* (S. Weber Nicholsen, Trans.). Minneapolis: University of Minnesota Press.

Hall, Stuart. (1988). *The Hard Road to Renewal.* London: Verso.

Hall, Stuart. (1991). *New Times: The Changing Face of Politics in the 1990s.* London: Routledge.

Hall, Stuart & Tony Jefferson (Eds.). (1990). *Resistance Through Rituals: Youth Subcultures in Postwar Britain.* London: Routledge. (This was originally published as Working Papers in Cultural Studies 7/8 from the Centre for Contemporary Cultural Studies at the University of Birmingham. For an in-depth study of Stuart Hall's work, see *Journal of Communication Inquiry,* Summer, 1986, which is devoted to him.)

Hall, Stuart & Paddy Whannel. (1967). *The Popular Arts: A Critical Guide to the Mass Media.* Boston, MA: Beacon Press.

Hartley, John. (1992). *The Politics of Pictures: The Creation of the Public in the Age of Popular Media.* London: Routledge.

Hartley, John. (1992). *Tele-ology: Studies in Television.* London: Routledge.

Haug, W.F. (1971). *Critique of Commodity Aesthetics: Appearance, Sexuality and Advertising in Capitalist Society* (R. Bock, Trans.). Minneapolis: University of Minnesota Press.
Haug, W.F. (1987). *Commodity Aesthetics, Ideology & Culture.* New York: International General.
Hoggart, Richard. (1992). *The Uses of Literacy.* New Brunswick, NJ: Transaction Books.
Hoover, Stewart M. (1988). *Mass Media Religion: The Social Sources of the Electronic Church.* Newbury Park, CA: Sage.
Hutcheon, Linda. (1989). *The Politics of Postmodernism.* London: Routledge.
Jacobs, Norman. (Ed.). (1992). *Mass Media in Modern Society.* New Brunswick, NJ: Transaction Books.
Jakobson, Roman. (1985). *Verbal Art, Verbal Sign, Verbal Time* (K. Pomorska & S. Rudy, Eds.). Minneapolis: University of Minnesota Press.
Jally, Sut & Justin Lewis. (1992). *Enlightened Racism: The Cosby Show, Audiences and the Myth of the American Dream.* Boulder, CO: Westview.
Jameson, Frederic. (1981). *The Political Unconscious.* Ithaca, NY: Cornell University Press.
Jameson, Frederic. (1991). *Postmodernism: Or the Cultural Logic of Late Capitalism.* Durham, NC: Duke University Press.
Jameson, Frederic. (1992). *The Geopolitical Aesthetic: Cinema and Space in the World System.* Bloomington: Indiana University Press.
Jameson, Frederic. (1992). *Signatures of the Visible.* New York: Routledge.
Jauss, Hans Robert. (1982). *Toward an Aesthetic of Reception* (T. Bahti, Trans.). Minneapolis: University of Minnesota Press.
Jensen, Joli. (1990). *Redeeming Modernity: Contradictions in Media Criticism.* Newbury Park, CA: Sage.
Jones, Ernest. (1949). *Hamlet and Oedipus.* New York: Norton.
Jones, Steve. (1992). *Rock Formation: Music, Technology and Mass Communication.* Thousand Oaks, CA: Sage.
Jones, Steven G. (Ed.). (1994). *Cybersociety: Computer-Mediated Communication and Community.* Thousand Oaks, CA: Sage.
Jowett, Garth & James M. Linton. (1989). *Movies as Mass Communication.* Newbury Park: Sage.
Jowett, Garth S. & Victoria O'Donnell. (1992). *Propaganda and Persuasion* (2nd ed.). Thousand Oaks, CA: Sage.
Jung, Carl G. (Ed.). (1968). *Man and His Symbols.* New York: Dell.
Kellner, Douglas. (1992). *The Persian Gulf TV War.* Boulder, CO: Westview.

Korzenny, Felix & Stella Ting-Toomey. (Eds.). (1992). *Mass Media Effects Across Cultures*. Newbury Park, CA: Sage.

Lacan, Jacques. (1966). *Ecrits: A Selection* (A. Sheridan, Trans.). New York: Norton.

Larsen, Neil. (1989). *Modernism and Hegemony: A Materialist Critique of Aesthetic Agencies*. Minneapolis: University of Minnesota Press.

Laurentis, Teresa de. (1984). *Alice Doesn't: Feminism, Semiotics, Cinema*. Bloomington: Indiana University Press.

Laurentis, Teresa de. (1987). *Technologies of Gender: Essays on Theory, Film and Fiction*. Bloomington: Indiana University Press.

Lazere, Donald. (Ed.). (1987). *America Media and Mass Culture: Left Perspectives*. Berkeley: University of California Press.

Lefebvre, Henri. (1984). *Everyday Life in the Modern World*. New Brunswick, NJ: Transaction Books.

Levi-Strauss, Claude. (1967). *Structural Anthropology*. Garden City, NY: Doubleday.

LeFebvre, Henri. (1984). *Everyday Life in the Modern World* (S. Rabinovitch, Trans.). New Brunswick, NJ: Transaction Books.

Levy, Mark R. & Michael Gurevitch. (Eds.). (1994). *Defining Media Studies: Reflections on the Future of the Field*. New York: Oxford University Press.

Lipsitz, George. (1989). *Time Passages: Collective Memory and American Popular Culture*. Minneapolis: University of Minnesota Press.

Lotman, Yuri M. (1976). *Semiotics of Cinema*. Ann Arbor: Michigan Slavic Contributions.

Lotman, Yuri M. (1977). *The Structure of the Artistic Text*. Ann Arbor: Michigan Slavic Contributions.

Lotman, Yuri M. (1991). *Universe of the Mind: A Semiotic Theory of Culture*. Bloomington: Indiana University Press.

MacCannell, Dean & Juliet Flower MacCannell. (1982). *The Time of the Sign: A Semiotic Interpretation of Modern Culture*. Bloomington: Indiana University Press.

MacDonald, J. Fred. (1994). *One Nation Under Television*. Chicago: Nelson-Hall.

Mattelart, Armand & Michele Mattelart. (1992). *Rethinking Media Theory* (J.A. Cohen & M. Urquidi, Trans.). Minneapolis: University of Minnesota Press.

Mandel, Ernest. (1985). *Delightful Murder: A Social History of the Crime Story*. Minneapolis: University of Minnesota Press.

McCarthy, Thomas. (1991). *Ideals and Illusions: On Reconstruction and Deconstruction in Contemporary Critical Theory*. Cambridge, MA: MIT Press.

McCue, Greg, with Clive Bloom. (1993). *Dark Knights: The New Comics in Context.* Boulder, CO: Westview.
McLuhan, Marshall. (1965). *Understanding Media: The Extensions of Man.* New York: McGraw-Hill.
McLuhan, Marshall. (1970). *Culture is Our Business.* New York: McGraw-Hill.
McLuhan, Marshall & Quentin Fiore. (1967). *The Medium is the Massage.* New York: Bantam Books.
McQuail, Denis. (1992). *Media Performance: Mass Communication and the Public Interest.* Thousand Oaks, CA: Sage.
McQuail, Denis. (1994). *Mass Communication Theory: An Introduction.* Thousand Oaks, CA: Sage.
Mellencamp, Patricia. (1990). *Indiscretions: Avant-Garde Film, Video and Feminism.* Bloomington: Indiana University Press.
Mellencamp, Patricia. (Ed.). (1990). *Logics of Television: Essays in Cultural Criticism.* Bloomington: Indiana University Press.
Messaris, Paul. (1994). *Visual Literacy: Image, Mind & Reality.* Boulder, CO: Westview Press.
Metz, Christian. (1982). *The Imaginary Signifier: Psychoanalysis and the Cinema* (C. Britton, Trans.). Bloomington: Indiana University Press.
Mindess, Harvey. (1971). *Laughter and Liberation.* Los Angeles: Nash.
Modleski, Tania. (1984). *Loving with a Vengeance: Mass-Produced Fantasies for Women.* New York: Routledge.
Modleski, Tania. (Ed.). (1986). *Studies in Entertainment: Critical Approaches to Mass Culture.* Bloomington: Indiana University Press.
Modleski, Tania. (1988). *The Women Who Knew Too Much: Hitchcock and Feminist Theory.* New York: Routledge.
Moores, Shaun. (1994). *Interpreting Audiences: The Ethnography of Media Consumption.* Thousand Oaks, CA: Sage.
Morley, David. (1988). *Family Television: Cultural Power and Domestic Leisure.* London: Routledge.
Morley, David. (1993). *Television Audiences and Cultural Studies.* London: Routledge.
Mulvey, Laura. (1989). *Visual and Other Pleasures.* Bloomington: Indiana University Press.
Nash, Christopher. (Ed.). (1990). *Narrative in Culture.* London: Routledge.
Navarro, Desiderio. (Ed.). (1993). Postmodernism: Center and Periphery. *The South Atlantic Quarterly.*
Nichols, Bill. (1981). *Ideology and the Image: Social Representation in the Cinema and Other Media.* Bloomington: Indiana University Press.

Nichols, Bill. (1992). *Representing Reality: Issues and Concepts in Documentary*. Bloomington: Indiana University Press.
Penley, Constance. (1989). *The Future of An Illusion: Film, Feminism and Psychoanalysis*. Minneapolis: University of Minnesota Press.
Phelan, James. (Ed.). (1989). *Reading Narrative: Form, Ethics, Ideology*. Columbus: Ohio State University Press.
Powell, Chris & George E.C. Paton (Eds.). (1988). *Humour in Society: Resistance and Control*. New York: St. Martin's Press.
Prindle, David. F. (1993). *Risky Business: The Political Economy of Hollywood*. Boulder, CO: Westview.
Propp, Vladimir. (1973). *Morphology of the Folk Tale* (2nd ed.). Austin: University of Texas Press.
Propp, Vladimir. (1984). *Theory and History of Folklore* (A.Y. Martin & R.P. Martin, Trans.). Minneapolis: University of Minnesota Press.
Ramet, Sabrina Petra. (Ed.). (1993). *Rocking the State: Rock Music and Politics in Eastern Europe and the Soviet Union*. Boulder, CO: Westview.
Reinelt, Janelle G. & Joseph R. Roach. (Eds.). (1993). *Critical Theory and Performance*. Ann Arbor: University of Michigan Press.
Richter, Mischa & Harald Bakken. (1992). *The Cartoonist's Muse: A Guide to Generating and Developing Creative Ideas*. Chicago: Contemporary Books.
Ryan, Michael & Douglas Kellner. (1988). *Camera Politica: The Politics and Ideology of Contemporary Hollywood Film*. Bloomington: Indiana University Press.
Sabin, Roger. (1993). *Adult Comics: An Introduction*. London: Routledge.
Schechner, Richard. (1993). *The Future of Ritual: Writings on Culture and Performance*. London: Routledge.
Schwichtenberg, Cathy. (Ed.). *The Madonna Collection*. Boulder, CO: Westview.
Schneider, Cynthia & Brian Wallis. (Eds.). (1989). *Global Television*. Cambridge, MA: MIT Press.
Schostak, John. (1993). *Dirty Marks: The Education of Self, Media and Popular Culture*. Boulder, CO: Westview.
Skovman, Michael. (Ed.). (undated). *Media Fictions*. Aarhus, DK: Aarhus University Press.
Sebeok, Thomas. (Ed.). (1978). *Sight, Sound and Sense*. Bloomington: Indiana University Press
Seldes, Gilbert. (1994). *The Public Arts*. New Brunswick, NJ: Transaction Books.
Shukman, Ann. (1977). *Literature and Semiotics: A Study of the Writings of Yuri M. Lotman*. Amsterdam: North-Holland.

Silverman, Kaja. (1983). *The Subject of Semiotics*. New York: Oxford University Press.
Smith, Gary. (Ed.). (1991). *On Walter Benjamin: Critical Essays and Recollections*. Cambridge, MA: MIT Press.
Steidman, Steven. (1993). *Romantic Longings: Love in America (1830-1980)*. New York: Routledge.
Stephenson, William. (1988). *The Play Theory of Mass Communication*. New Brunswick, NJ: Transaction Books.
Szondi, Peter. (1986). *On Textual Understanding* (H. Mendelsohn, Trans.). Minneapolis: University of Minnesota Press.
Todorov, Tzvetan. (1975). *The Fantastic: A Structural Approach to a Literary Genre* (R. Howard, Trans.). Ithaca, NY: Cornell University Press.
Todorov, Tzvetan. (1981). *Introduction to Poetics* (R. Howard, Trans.). Minneapolis: University of Minnesota Press.
Traube, Elizabeth G. (1982). *Dreaming Identities: Class, Gender, and Generation in the 1980s Hollywood Movies*. Boulder, CO: Westview.
Turner, Bryan S. (1990). *Theories of Modernity and Postmodernity*. London: Sage.
Van Zoonen, Liesbet. (1994). *Feminist Media Studies*. Thousand Oaks, CA: Sage.
Volosinov, V.N. (1987). *Freudianism: A Critical Sketch* (I.R. Titunik, Trans.). Bloomington: Indiana University Press.
Weibel, Kathryn. (1977). *Mirror Mirror: Images of Women Reflected in Popular Culture*. Garden City, NY: Anchor Books.
Wernick, Andrew. (1991). *Promotional Culture*. London: Sage.
Willemen, Paul. (1993). *Looks and Frictions: Essays in Cultural Studies and Film Theory*. Bloomington: Indiana University Press.
Williams, Raymond. (1958). *Culture and Society: 1780-1950*. New York: Columbia University Press.
Williams, Raymond. (1976). *Keywords*. New York: Oxford University Press.
Williams, Raymond. (1977). *Marxism and Literature*. New York: Oxford University Press.
Williams, Rosalind. (1990). *Notes on the Underground: An Essay on Technology, Society and the Imagination*. Cambridge, MA: MIT Press.
Williamson, Judith. (1978). *Decoding Advertisements: Ideology and Meaning in Advertising*. London: Marion Boyars.
Willis, Paul. (1990). *Common Culture: Symbolic Work at Play in the Everyday Cultures of the Young*. Boulder, CO: Westview.

Wilson, Clint C. & Felix Gutierrez. (1985). *Minorities and Media: Diversity and the End of Mass Communication.* Thousand Oaks, CA: Sage.

Winick, Charles. (1994). *Desexualization in American Life: The New People.* New Brunswick, NJ: Transaction Books.

Wollen, Peter. (1972). *Signs and Meaning in the Cinema.* Bloomington: Indiana University Press.

Wollen, Peter. (1993). *Raiding the Icebox: Reflections on Twentieth-Century Culture.* Bloomington: Indiana University Press.

Wright, Will. (1975). *Sixguns and Society: A Structural Study of the Western.* Berkeley: University of California Press.

Zizek, Slavoi. (1991). *Looking Awry: An Introduction to Jacques Lacan through Popular Culture.* Cambridge, MA: MIT Press.

# *Index*

Abrams, M.H., 19, *147*
Advertising agencies, 93-135
*Adweek*, 99
*All in the Family*, 39
Angell, David, 59
Aristotle, 19, 57

*Bald Soprano,* 65, 76
Ball, Kim, 105
Berger, Arthur Asa, 7, 37, 54, 94, 140, 141, *147*
Berger, Peter, 134, *147*
*Beverly Hillbillies,* 39
Bloom, Allan, 31, *147*
Bloopers, 67-80
    ethical problems in using, 71-72
    kinds of, 67-68
    why we laugh at, 68-69
Bon, Gustav Le, 29
*Bonanza,* 39
Borges, Jorge Luis, 72, *147*
Brennan, Barbara, 95
Byrne, David, 11

Capone, Al, 79
Capp, Al, 138, 139
Carek, Paul, 101

Casey, Peter, 59
*Celestial Emporium of Benevolent Knowledge*, 72
*Cheers,* 65
Chun, Gaynor Strachan, 99
Churchill, Winston, 107
Cigarette smoking, 81-84
    ritualistic aspects of, 82-84
    as theater, 83
Clarke, Andrew, 107, 108
Claude Lévi-Strauss, 84
Codes in college classrooms, 89-91
    boredom of students, 91
    lurkers in distance learning courses, 91
    student–professor relationships chart, 89
    student use of passive aggression, 90
Cognitive dissonance, 36
Concepts, 15
    defined, 29
    impact on people, 29-30
*Consumer Culture and Postmodernism*, 41
*Consumer Reports*, 103

Culture
    behavior patterns, 9
    embodied in artifacts, 10
    meanings of term, 8-10
    socially acquired traits, 9
    tied to human groups, 10
    transmission by symbols, 9-10
de Certeau, M., 24, *147*
Douglas, Stuart, 120
Doyle, Dave, 102, 103-104
Eco, Umberto, 140
*Ed Sullivan Show*, 39
English advertising agency, 122-135
    advertising follows, doesn't lead, 133-134
    Bisto, 123, 134
    cigarette advertising, 124
    importance of bad taste, 133
    Martell cognac, 130-133
    problem of research, 128
    role of creative directors, 124-125
    turnover of employees, 126
*Falling Off the Map: Some Lonely Places of the World*, 10-12
Faulkner, William, 40
Featherstone, Mike, 41, *147*
Finnegan's Wake, 39
*Frasier*, 57-65
    analogies, 64
    before and after humor, 61
    cataloging, 61
    comic definition, 60
    comic exaggeration, 60
    comic insults in, 61
    eccentricity humor, 60
    mistakes, 61
    repartee, 62
    revelation of character, 63
    reversal humor, 63
    role of fools in, 57
    techniques of humor, 59
    "The Good Son" episode, 59-64
    theories of humor, 58
Freud, Sigmund, 5, 57
Fulbright, William, 53
Gandhi, Mahatma, 72
Gans, Herbert, 37-40, 41, *147*

*Genesis,* 23
Gilbert, Kimberly, 115, 116
Gilliam, Mary Beth, 108-109
Girard, René, 21, 22, *147*
Goldberg, Fred, 93, 95, 99, 118, 119
Goldberg, Max, 137
Goldberg Moser O'Neill, 93-121
    advertising for drama queens, 108
    Boston Market campaign, 110-111, 112
    branding people, 96
    brand planners, 107
    changing perceptions via advertising, 116-117
    Cisco campaign brand promise, 114-115
    Cisco commercials, 98-99
    Cisco Systems campaign, 120-121
    Citra campaign, 100-101
    Dreyer's ice cream commercial, 109
    importance of emotions in ads, 102
    Kia campaign, 103-104
    reasons for bad advertising, 112-114
Grossman, Ruth, 94

*Hamlet*, 7, 8
*Hamlet Case,* 94
*Harper's*, 39
*Harper's Index,* 25
Hawthorne, Nathaniel, 40
Hemingway, Ernest, 40
Henderson, Joseph, 19
Hill, Nancy, 106
Hip-hop music, 31
Hobbes, Thomas, 57
Huizinga, J., 81, *147*

Identification with symbolic heroes and heroines, 15
    halo effect from identification, 18
    identification defined, 18
*Ideology and Utopia,* 4
*Il Mulino* magazine, 140
*I Love Lucy,* 39
Images, 15, 22-23
Information, 15, 23-24
Ionesco, Eugene, 58, 65
Iyer, Pico, 10, *147*

# INDEX

Johnson, Mark, 16, *147*
Jonson, Ben, 65
Joyce, James, 40
Jung, Carl, 19
Kant, Immanuel, 57
Kerr, Alan, 120-121
Lakoff, George, 16, *147*
*Lawrence Welk Show,* 39
Leach, Edmund, 84, 84-86, *148*
Le Bon, 29, *148*
Lee, David, 59
Lévi-Strauss, Claude, 84, 86
*Life,* 39
*Li'l Abner,* 37, 137-141
    Shmoos, 138
    as subject of PhD dissertation, 137-141
*Li'l Abner: A Study in American Satire,* 140
Listwin, Don, 120
Lull, James, 30, *148*
Lyotard, Jean-François, 41, 42, *148*
MacIntosh "1984" commercial, 99
MacIver, Ian, 137
Mannheim, Karl, 4, *148*
Marx, Karl, 50
*Mary Tyler Moore Show,* 39
*Mass Comm Murders,* 141
McAuliffe, Catrina, 94, 97, 118
Media, 20-21
    focal points in study of, 20
    theories of art and, 20
Meehan, Chuck, 102
Melaga, Tito, 117
Melville, Herman, 40
Metaphors, 15, 16-18
    importance in everyday life, 16
    love is a game, 16-18
*Metaphors We Live By,* 16
Mimesis, 15
    definition of, 19
    theories of art and, 19-20
Mimetic desire, 15
    defined, 21-22
    in Shakespeare's plays, 22
*Mirror and the Lamp: Romantic Theory and the Critical Tradition,* 19

Models we imitate, 15, 22
Moser, Mike, 93, 114-115
Mowat, Matt, 102, 103
Music, 15
    impact on consciousness of people, 30
    importance of rhythm, 31
    power of, 30-32
*Newsweek,* 39
*New Yorker,* 26, 39
Nietzel, John, 119-120
Noble, David, 138
O'Neill, Brian, 93
O'Rourke, Dennis, 97
*Other Inquisitions,* 72
Plautus, 58
Pokémon, 23
Political cultures, 33
    egalitarians, 34-37
    elitists, 34-37
    fatalists, 35-37
    four basic ones, 34-37
    individualists, 35-37
Popular, 6-8
Popular culture, 1-13
    contrast with elite culture, 7
    impact on personality, 15-28
*Popular Culture and High Culture,* 37
*Popular Music and Communication,* 30
*Positioning: The Battle for Your Mind,* 111
*Postmodern Condition: A Report on Knowledge,* 41
Postmodernism, 33
    attack on absolutes, 41
    defined, 41-42
    importance of narratives, 42
*Postmortem for a Postmodernist,* 94, 141
*Practice of Everyday Life,* 24
*Psychology Today,* 39
Quennell, Brian, 116, 117
*Reader's Digest,* 39
Real, Michael, 55, *148*
Reinforcement, 37-38
Repetition compulsion, 5-6
Reykjavik, 11-12
Rietta, Terry, 112-114

# INDEX

Rios, A., 111, *148*
Robbins, Harold, 39
Rock music, 31
Rockwell, Norman, 39
Saigon, 10-11
*Saturday Evening Post*, 39
Saussure, Ferdinand, de, 23, 29, *148*
Semiotics
    images and, 23
    people reading, 23
    signifiers and signifieds, 23
Shakespeare, William, 7, 21, 58, 65, 71
Shubert, Jeff, 98
Sibley, Mulford Q., 138
*Society*, 141
Socrates, 31
Spectacles, 15, 29
Stoppard, Tom, 65
Stories, 15
    jokes as narratives, 25-28
    Tan joke analysis, 26-28
Stout, Jack, 111, *148*
Super Bowl, 47-55
    cost of commercials, 51
    cultural imperialism, 51
    linguistic analysis of term, 49-50
    Marxist view of, 50-51
    psychoanalytic perspectives on, 53-54
    semiotic analysis of, 52
    sociological aspects of, 54-55
    violence in, 53
*Superman*, 18
Supermarkets, 87-89
    as labyrinths, 87
    routes used in, 87-88

*Survivor*, 24, 40
Symbolic heroes and heroines
    identification, 18-19
    socialization by, 19
Taste cultures, 33
    high culture, 38
    low culture, 38
    lower middle culture, 38
    quasi-folk low culture, 38-39
    upper middle culture, 38
Tennyson, Alfred Lord, 75
*Theater of Envy*, 21
*Time*, 39
Traffic signals, 84-86
*Transaction*, 141
*Travesties*, 65
*Twelfth Night*, 65
*20-20* television show, 119
University of Iowa, 137
University of Massachusetts, 137
University of Milan, 140
*Volpone*, 65
*Waning of the Middle Ages*, 81
*Washington Post*, 47, 138
*Wayne's World*, 7
*Who Wants to be a Millionaire*, 40
Wildavsky, Aaron, 34, 35, 36, 39
*Wonder Woman*, 18
Woods, Tiger, 18
Wordsworth, William, 75, 76
Yarnold, Yvonne, 95, 96
Young, Marguerite, 138
Young, Patti, 110-111